Courtly Love in the Shopping Mall

Humanities Programming
for Young Adults

Created by
Evelyn Shaevel
and
Peggy O'Donnell

Edited by
Susan Goldberg
and
Rolly Kent

American Library
Association
Chicago and London
1991

The material on which this book is based was developed
by Evelyn Shaevel and Peggy O'Donnell for the Young Adult Services
Division of the American Library Association with funding
from the National Endowment for the Humanities.

Text and cover designed by Margo Burwell

Cover illustration by Mary Phelan
based on a photograph by Margo Burwell

Composed by The Clarinda Company in Palatino text
with Chancery display on a Xyvision system
using a Linotron 202 typesetter

Printed on 50-pound Glatfelter, a pH-neutral stock,
and bound in 10-point Carolina cover stock
by Edwards Brothers, Inc.

The paper used in this publication meets the minimum requirements of American National Standard for Information Sciences—Permanence of Paper for Printed Library Materials, ANSI Z39.48-1984. ∞

Illustrations in *Courtly Love in the Shopping Mall* are taken
from *The Blue Fairy Book,* edited by Andrew Lange (1889; reprint,
New York: Dover, 1965), and *The Red Fairy Book,* edited by
Andrew Lang (New York: Longmans, 1922).

Library of Congress Cataloging-in-Publication Data

Shaevel, Evelyn.
    Courtly love in the shopping mall : humanities programming for
young adults / created by Evelyn Shaevel and Peggy O'Donnell :
edited by Susan Goldberg and Rolly Kent.
        p.   cm.
    Includes index.
    ISBN 0-8389-3387-4
    1. Libraries, Young people's—Activity programs.   2. Libraries and
education—United States.   3. Young adults—Books and reading.
4. Humanities—Study and teaching.   5. Young adults—Education.
I. O'Donnell, Peggy.   II. Goldberg, Susan, 1944–   .   III. Kent,
Rolly.   IV. Title.
Z718.5.S5   1990   90-44211
027.8'223—dc20

95 94 93 92 91   5 4 3 2 1

ontents

8 ◆ A Second Possibility for Further Humanities Programming 108

Introduction

In 1985, the Young Adult Services Division (YASD) of the American Library Association was awarded a major grant from the National Endowment for the Humanities (NEH) to train librarians who work with young adults to design and implement humanities programs. The training was done in a series of regional workshops held over a two-year period across the United States. The participants in the workshops were composed of teams of three people—a librarian who works with young adults, a library administrator, and a humanities scholar. The teams came from public and school libraries. The workshops provided librarians with the basic information and knowledge to approach the study of the humanities and the practical skills necessary to develop proposals for humanities programs in a library-sponsored setting—programs that would introduce the humanities to young adults by bringing together the young adult and the humanities scholar.

The workshops focused on three areas: an introduction to the humanities, instruction in the design and preparation of proposals to develop humanities programming for young people, and a demonstration of model humanities programs. Most of the learning materials for the workshop were combined in a red notebook that was distributed to the participants.

The red notebook evolved over three years into a compilation of resources that could be used by anyone who wanted to present humanities programs. It provided a basic introduction to the humanities, to the concept of library programming, and to working with and developing programs for young adults. The notebook became a tool that workshop participants could use back home to lead them through the collaborative process of creating humanities programs in their libraries for young adults. We realized how useful this information was and wanted to share what we had learned with a much larger audience.

This book, *Courtly Love in the Shopping Mall: Humanities Programming for Young Adults,* is a direct descendant of that red notebook. We hope that you will use it to lead you through the process of understanding, planning, developing, and presenting humanities programs in libraries for young adults. But the book is only a tool. In the end, it is you—the librarian, teacher, or youth worker—who can most effectively bring together the scholar, the humanities, and the young adult. Librarians are the integral and integrating factors in the process of library programs in the humanities for young adults.

The title *Courtly Love in the Shopping Mall* came about as a result of an intense discussion between librarians and scholars. Scholar Brenda Murphy was asked to develop an idea comparing rituals of courtship for teenagers through the ages—from Shakespeare's time to today—for a demonstration program to be used at the training workshops. After a great deal of lively give and take about how to make this idea enticing to young people and what to call the program, librarian Susan Madden, former coordinator of young adult services at the King County (Washington) Public Library System, mentioned that shopping malls were the places teenagers went to meet the opposite sex. Joan Atkinson, associate professor at the University of Alabama Graduate School of Library Science, made the link and came up with "Courtly Love in the Shopping Mall." Murphy agreed and the collaborative process of program design was begun. You can see the results of Murphy's work in chapter 3 of this book.

As our title suggests, we are interested in humanities and library programming as ways to bring young people into contact with each other and with the rest of the world. Love, one of the mighty concerns of young people, which, so we are told, keeps all people young, brings two or more people into sometimes amazing states of being: it shocks, scares, astounds, and delights—sometimes all at once. Of course, young people have many other concerns—war and destruction; boredom; identity; honesty; reality; and so on the list rolls. But we choose *love* and *shopping* as the evocative words because they seem so unconnected, so . . . well . . . opposite, as if they would cancel each other out. Yet it is the paradoxical nature of life that has intrigued thinking people most; the man or woman, no matter the age, who can wrestle the angel of paradox wins a great blessing indeed. And that tussling with questions, with value, with meaning, is what makes the humanities, not to mention experience itself, quite an adventure. It is with the spirit of such a quest that we offer this guide to creating humanities programs in your library.

This book is written primarily for librarians who work with young adults in either public or school library settings, but it can be used as well by educators in middle, junior high, and high schools and community colleges and staff members of youth services organizations, museums, historical societies, and arts groups. And because the concepts and themes are so universal, we hope that any librarian who would like to develop humanities programs in her library will use the book to help her get started. Its aim is to help the reader understand the humanities and the potential role of humanities programming for young adults in his institution, plan and implement humanities programs, and develop and write proposals for funding for humanities programs. Additionally, we have included three sample programs that have been developed by the scholars and librarians who presented the YASD/NEH workshops. These demonstration programs can be used by the reader as a program for her library or as an aid in helping her understand the concept and process of humanities programming for youth. For the reader's convenience, we have also included a glossary of frequently used terms in the Appendixes section.

We hope you use this book as a workbook, an idea book, and a jumping-off point for your own programs for young people.

EVELYN SHAEVEL

cknowledgments
◆◆◆◆◆◆◆◆◆◆

We started the YASD/NEH Project at 50 East Huron Street, ALA Headquarters in Chicago, on a very cold weekend in December 1985 and have traveled many miles to bring our message about humanities programs and kids to librarians and scholars around the country. None of this would have been possible without the creativity, dedication, commitment, sense of humor, and tolerance of the YASD/NEH Project Advisory Committee. Many thanks and much credit goes to principal consultant Peggy O'Donnell; to project scholars Michael Bell, Brenda Murphy, Gregory Stevens, and Jamil Zainaldin; to librarians Joan Atkinson, Susan Goldberg, Susan Madden, and Mary K. Chelton; to NEH staff Tom Phelps, David Martz, and Bridget Bradley; and to ALA staff Marie Louise Settem and Catherine Moore—all of whom participated in the development of the project and all of whom were cast at one time or another in our traveling road show, bringing this project, this book, and humanities programs for young adults to life! Not only did we learn a great deal from one another about libraries, young adults, and humanities, but we had lots of fun in the process. Thank you to all of the librarians and scholars who attended our workshops in Madison, Wisconsin; Pomona and San Francisco, California; Austin, Texas; Durham, New Hampshire; St. Augustine, Florida; and Philadelphia, Pennsylvania. For their vision and encouragement, the YASD officers and board of directors, who supported the concept and the project from the start, have my gratitude.

Without Peggy O'Donnell, Susan Goldberg, and Rolly Kent, this book would never have been created, let alone completed. Sally Estes, Stephanie Zvirin, and Hazel Rochman of *Booklist* magazine created wonderful bibliographies that have added much to the project, and Sally Mason and Irene Wood shared their knowledge of film and video. Ann Carlson Weeks, Susan Horiuchi, and Tina MacAyeal provided a fresh perspective and insight into this enduring endeavor.

And finally, a special thank you to Will, who inspired me to action when he said, "Stop crying and go write a grant proposal!" So that's what Peggy and I did. Now, five years later, you are holding the ultimate product of the YASD/NEH Project in your hands.

EVELYN SHAEVEL

1 ♦ Introducing Humanities Programming for Young Adults

f you are familiar with library programming, you know that the drama of human interaction, especially young adult interaction, has a much different reality than that created by the relationship between reader and printed page. Within the context of this book, we will constantly be referring you from the book to the human arena of programming.

This book works like a triple helix. In it, we will be assuming that the separate threads of *programming, young adults,* and *the humanities* are an integral, integrated unity in the world beyond the page. Before we talk about the why and how-to, though, let's first examine each of these three threads. Then we will wind them back around one another and discuss the special nature of humanities programming for young adults.

The thrust of this book is to respond to the challenge of helpfulness with practical measures. The concept of the library program is central to this challenge. The artificial world of the book must transform into the world in which you and your clientele, your audience—young adults—exist with that delirium and mystery that is teenage life.

What Is a Program?

Because libraries are public places, for years they have organized all sorts of public events, from children's story hours to voter registration drives to classes in folk dancing. Really, library programming is an extension of more traditional, book-bound information service. Programming extends the concept of the book as a resource for self-education and amusement to people themselves. In programming, learning and entertainment (and the line between these two is often quite thin) are not limited to checking out books, but rather are broadened to include the book as just one form of communication and learning. Simply put, all library programming, however modest, is part of the library's mission in lifelong learning, implicit both in library traditions and the nature of books themselves.

A program is a form of publication; it is a way of making something—anything—public. Good library programs can and ought to include traditional media through which people have transmitted information, be that information regarding Truth or about how to prepare the best meals. Humans are still consumers of information needed to both act and think. No matter how young people are seen to change by their elders, people will always need to learn how to focus their minds, how to brave the infinite changes of heart that are in store for all, and how to use and enjoy the energy of the body and the material world about them.

For the purposes of this book and for planning and implementing humanities programs for young people, it will be worth our time to think in large and (of course!) humanistic terms about this notion of the program. Really, a program is a response to our need to learn and our need to be part of a community. Whether it is a storytelling time, a dance class, a lecture in molecular physics, a public forum on nuclear disarmament or censorship, or an informational meeting on voter registration or literacy, there is an art to creating good programs, programs that go beyond scheduling meeting room space. A good program provides an opportunity for people not only to get together, but to interact. For humanities programming, our cause, it is a chance to get people thinking together.

So good programs make room for people to meet, interact, think, share. They inspire going further—often, paradoxically, by asking a question that is answered with the next question—sometimes to pursue individual study, sometimes to return to another session of a multi-meeting program.

In a sense, programming is also a form of education as well as publication. We want to learn, and we want to learn together, in public. One useful way to grasp the significance of programming is to see a program as a chance for people to "publish" their thoughts through the give and take of talking, listening, thinking, reading, observing, and doing—together. The results are often not tangible, so one of the first lessons in understanding programs is that they do not depend on tests, papers, or other evaluative outcomes. The medium is the message, Marshall McLuhan wrote nearly 30 years ago. To participate is the real "product." Or, really, the procedure of thinking together is what matters most.

In addition, good programs recognize the nature, personality, or level that the audience of participants reflects. Especially with young adults, who are practically change embodied, program creators have to be alert and tuned in to the special nuances and particularities of teenage thought, feeling, and experience.

What Is a Young Adult and Why Young Adult Services?

The traditional definition of *young adult* in most libraries is young people in junior and senior high school, roughly between twelve and eighteen years old. A definition often used by librarians and others who work with youth states that a young adult is a person in transition who no longer sees himself or herself as a child, but who is not yet an adult. As stated in a classic YASD publication, *Directions for Library Service to Young Adults* (ALA, 1977):

> . . . Psychologists agree that there is a set of universal tasks that must be mastered during this transition period; the adolescent must achieve emotional, social, and intellectual maturity; independence from parents; adult attitudes toward sex; occupational goals; satisfactory uses of leisure; [and perhaps most important in relation to involvement in humanities programs] philosophy of life; and self-identity. These tasks are assumed at a time when biological changes are more likely than not to cause anxiety. In attempting to cope with these stresses, adolescents become unpredictable, frequently vacillating between the old childish behavior patterns and experimenting with adult models. Strain between them and adults is almost inevitable, for while adolescents feel compelled to challenge authority figures in order to flex fledgling wings of independence, the insecure state of their psyches makes them extremely vulnerable and sensitive to adult criticism, real or imagined. . . .

Within this context, the goal of library service for young adults is to aid the individual in achieving a successful transition from childhood to adulthood by providing the resources and the environment that will foster intellectual, emotional, and social development. . . . Reaching young adults, both within and outside the library; stimulating and delighting them with the discovery of good books, films, music, art—all the best fruits of human endeavor; motivating them to extend their knowledge and broaden their horizons; encouraging positive and creative interests; developing their ability to seek information required for intelligent decision making; . . . helping them to accept the responsibility of living in a complex world—these are, in essence, the purpose of work with this age group.

What Is Humanities Programming?

We humans are odd creatures. We have a capacity that singles us out from our fellow creatures with whom we share the planet. We have the ability to study ourselves, to ask, and potentially to know, who we are.

"Who am I?" That is the question the Sphinx asked. Fortunately, the Sphinx left some clues. At the outset of our book about humanities programming for libraries, we might very well ask a similar sphinx question: What *are* the humanities, anyway? Certainly, the word itself contains the answer—the humanities are what make us humans. Like our fellow creatures the animals, we possess the ability to travel and move. We eat, and we provide food. Like our fellow creatures, we train our young in the ways of survival.

But depending on how we are taught to view such things, our ability to move becomes a human passion for freedom or a fascination with home, mother, the natural environment, or the nation, with memory of places and times when we were young. And we eat, but we like to eat what tastes good, and we make a ritual out of preparing the food, including buying it at the store. Fewer and fewer people have to run down, trap, or kill their food directly; we have societies of varying complexity that include people whose place it is to make the food for us so we can get it, and this structuring has led to very complex economies and further complexities of social life. And perhaps most uniquely, our systems of transmitting information about the collective knowledge of being human have become marvelously rich, diverse, baffling, and frightening.

For we are the creatures who have self-awareness. We know we are people. We remember. We talk. We write, film, videotape, computerize. Our dogs and cats love us, even understand what we say to them, but they can't remember to turn on the pot roast at 5 o'clock or water the lawn at dawn. They can't look back on the birth of their first children with sweetness or cry because the kids have all left home. Our fellow creatures the animals do not know who they are, where they've come from, or what their dreams and fears are. Their lives are factual; the dog knows that she lives at home, that she belongs with the house and its other occupants, that whatever smells like her is part of her, and that she wants to eat, wants to sleep, wants to run.

The roles of memory and intellect are extremely important for us. Our lives are capable of more than factual limits because of these mental facilities. We can miniaturize all of human experience and carry it around with us. We can remember, and we can recite, view works of art, and read literature, history, and philosophy. We can study ourselves and make changes in the way we do things without needing to undergo generations of evolutionary development in order to effect change at a biological and genetic level. The Siberian Husky whose ancestors lived in the Arctic still loves to pull even though she was born and raised in the desert.

The humanities, then, are all the disciplines of study that focus on what makes us human. But also as noteworthy, the humanities imply a style of study. The humanist is one who asks questions, all of which lead further into the deepening understanding of what is human. Who am I? Why do I live? These are questions whose answers are themselves lifelong journeying, and for every answer the humanist finds for a question, this new answer leads to a new question, and thus the humanist is on a journey into both his origins in the earth and his hunger for stars.

The humanist is not a man or woman apart from the world, but—as Wallace Stevens, the American poet, put it—an adventurer in humanity. The adventure. Not something intellectual and unemotional. For the humanist, the world is a place capable of surprises— otherwise, he or she already knows the answer. The humanist, paradoxically, loves the question nearly as much as the answer. The humanist follows the labyrinth to its innermost nub, like a person unwinding an onion, following the endless curve of peeling as it unwinds from the layer below it, one layer after another of question-mark-shaped peeling.

One of the demands placed on cultural institutions is to teach what is of value from our collective knowledge and experience in ways that the young can truly hear. This is no easy task for any generation of adults. We almost have to trick ourselves into the truth.

How do we pass on to our young the love, the passion for knowing? How shall we convince them of the need for thought? How will we adults, especially we who are formally and loosely part of the educational and library professions, help the young understand the richness, diversity, and ever-changing nature of life? What would help them live with awareness of themselves and their place in time?

People working in educational institutions and libraries have been trained to place a special value on language as it is presented to us in written form. But, as many of us realize, human culture is expressed in many more ways than the written word. We adults, dedicated to the value of humanistic thinking and the role of libraries and education in modern life, are committed to helping young people master the intricacies of thinking for themselves. But, on the other hand, it is only fair that we who are older do not overlook the amazing cultural panoply that teens today navigate quite as well as Odysseus sailed his seas. Video, stereos, compact discs, computer-generated graphics, Nintendo, movies, radio, television, VCRs—these are additional venues for the expression of culture.

Would anyone in Homer's time have imagined committing the epic of Odysseus to anything other than memory? But by Shakespeare's time, one could read Homer in a book, thanks to the innovation of movable type and book printing. Likewise, Shakespeare probably couldn't have conceived of a film version of *Henry V* or of computer-generated text, although both these great bards knew that the human capacity to tell, to listen, *to create,* was immutable.

In our time, there are many ways in which our culture has created the means for destroying itself. The spear, the cannon, and the boat were early innovations of war making. Today, we have more insidious ways of destruction: the breakdown of family values and structures; drug alteration of our minds; loneliness caused by a sense of not belonging to a community; and television that both connects people into a global village and disconnects them from participation in their local neighborhood, village, or town.

Parents now rely on education to train young people about the ways and means of today's culture, a world governed more and more by abstract laws instead of word-of-mouth lessons and stories given us by elders of our tribes or clans. The ways in which young Americans are connected to a teenage cultural group mind are increasingly turned over to media that, by their nature, require very little physical and mental response: rock and roll music; television, with its powerful appeal to image and style; and movies, with their ready-made images that replace active imagination. . . . We don't have to do much work to watch or listen, so it has become easy and habitual to expect to be entertained.

Human beings cannot help making themselves part of a public or a group, something that is a bigger context than the merely personal and ego centered. We adults have gone through that powerful need to be part of a group, and we know it still holds a powerful sway over us. The humanities disciplines ask us to take control of what goes in and out of our minds. That is no longer such a simple task or skill to acquire as life becomes more and more complicated and subtle. How do we own our minds, our intellects? Is that important? Do kids need to be encouraged to "know thyself"? Library and school programs with humanities as their content all have the same response to this last question: yes, it is important to the quality of our world and our happiness to know ourselves.

In a talk to participants at the YASD/NEH training workshops, Gregory Stevens, assistant dean, College of Humanities and Fine Arts, SUNY, Albany, eloquently addressed this general thematic need to respond to the times through humanities programming.

The tools and raw materials of the humanities rest solidly in language. Greek "literature," in the widest sense, is wordy; nothing is simply put, except for Spartan epigrams ("son—[come home] with your shield or on it," Plutarch *Moralia* 2Y1F). The question is why? In the answer, we have, I think, the substance of humanities programming. One analogy made in the *Odyssey* is that between Odysseus and the epic poet. The Greek word *poet* means a maker, a maker of words in an order. It is a power in which we all share. It is a sense of accomplishment; a sense of making the external world ours.

Our conceptualization of the world and relationships in it would be difficult to imagine without words, discourse, the predication for our sense of a shareable community. Anne Sexton said it best in her poem "Words": "Sometimes I fly like an eagle but with the wings of a wren. /But I try to take care and be gentle to them. Words and eggs must be handled with care. /Once broken they are impossible things to repair." Odysseus doesn't exist except for the poet's memory. The user of language gives life to everything: people, things, ideas. The importance of the conscious act of utterance can be appreciated best in a formula from the Homeric epics: When something untoward is said, the question is asked, "What have you let escape the barrier of your teeth?" Odysseus, on one of his stops, listens to a poet recite verses about the Trojan War and he cries, "Why?" The poet has made the event itself more real than the actual experience. Moreover, we wish to hear: Odysseus has to hear the Sirens—like Oedipus, he has to know.

The power of words in human discourse is enormous. It translates our ideas and feelings into a common, remarkable form. The *Odyssey* and the humanities generically and characteristically do this. They are emancipatory: they free us from a preoccupation with our own affairs, the life of "unthinking servants" (from the federal legislation establishing NEH) or of the unknown citizen (compare the Greek notion of the specialist, the "idiot" in Thucydides, fifth-century B.C.: the person who is totally absorbed with his own affairs and who does not participate in the life of the polis is, pejoratively, a private person; or compare G. B. Shaw's maxim: "No man can be a pure specialist without being in the strict sense an idiot" in the "Revolutionist's Handbook," *Man and Superman*).

The humanities pull us away from our preferences to stay the same, to stay in one place, to maintain the unexamined life (compare the Socratic method of inquiry: "Ta ti," what is it?). I think this is what Shelley meant when he said we are all Greeks. We insist that life should be more than a quantitative amassing of possessions, or even days. Achilles makes the ultimate choice of value when he wishes for the short, active, glorious life instead of the long, uneventful one.

Similarly to the poet, the humanist takes the event, personage, book, sculpture, symphony, treatise, video, film, CD, and makes it more meaty by exercising the humanist's skills of analysis (what are the functions of Odysseus' trip to the Underworld to visit the dead?); of synthesis (the Greeks set one day aside each month for worshipping the dead—what do modern cultures do?); and of evaluation (what values are reflected in a society's treatment of the dead?). Moreover, why did Homer bother to compose 27,000 lines of poetry? Why did the culture keep the works alive orally for centuries? Responsibly, the humanist, through extensive training, provides the background, the context for beginning the discussion, the requisite specula and lenses.

Perhaps one way to capture what the humanist does is to use an analogy. I have chosen the prism because rainbows are one of my favorite things. Each humanist is a special prism: as he or she is asked to see and respond in language and the refraction that takes place gives out a whole spectrum of interpretation, whole new ways of seeing (the Greek stem *the* deals with "seeing": theory and theater). The humanist is trained to interpret, assess, weigh, and present several points of view through language and to facilitate the establishment of a diverse field of vision that allows others to share their seeing. That is what research in the humanities entails: researching, interpreting, communicating. It is within the continuities of that tradition that the humanities are made vital, if not for content, then for seeing how ideas are articulated.

The questions, the search for truth remain the same for each generation; the answers change as do the processes of asking. On a global level now, the humanist has easy access to materials that can be forged in new ways for public programming. For this and several reasons, humanists need to be more involved in American life, life beyond the academy. The National Endowment for the Humanities has done more to stimulate this partnership than any other agency. Some of us have already made a commitment to the humanities and humanities programming. But from my point of view there are too many undiscovered humanists and this should change, mainly because the humanist has a great deal to offer. A light under a bushel is of little solace in these overwrought times.

2 ♦ Creating Programs

man whose heart is set against love, the poet Ezra Pound wrote, will not be won over by love poems. It is probably true that anyone whose mind is already closed is not going to be enthused about the pleasures of thought and talk, two things that most humanities programs really are all about. It is easy to imagine how lonely the world would be without the interactions of people in love or people in thought. It would be best to help young people be strong enough to keep their hearts and minds open in the service of their own humanity. And thus we must somewhere or other open the case, take out the trumpet, and announce the start of our quest— whether that quest is for the holiest of holies or merely for a piece of paper to jot down items on a shopping list.

Library programming for young adults (generally defined as young people ages twelve to eighteen) is not a new idea. Many librarians have been providing summer reading programs, film showings, reading and discussion groups, booktalks, crafts demonstrations, and a variety of other programs for years. Most of these libraries have found that their programs are popular with young adults. For too many librarians, however, programming is still an untried task. A lack of funds and an already overworked staff have often prevented libraries from planning and producing programs. Some librarians hesitate because they have had little or no experience in designing programs. Others refrain from putting on programs because they fear it would be difficult to attract young people.

If your library has not yet sponsored young adult programs, whatever the reason, this chapter and following chapters will be of help to you. We will take you through all the steps of designing and staffing a program. We will advise you on how to get other people as well as community and youth groups to share the work of planning and producing a program. We will show you how to promote your program to draw the kind of audience you are looking for. And we will introduce you to the National Endowment for the Humanities (NEH), a federal agency that provides funding for library programs including out-of-school programs for youth who are uniquely suited to the goals of libraries.

As you read through this section, we hope you will be inspired to embark on a new and exciting venture for your library. We won't pretend that programming does not involve a lot of hard work, but we are sure that you will not be disappointed with the benefits for your community, staff, and library.

Why You Should Have Programs

Almost every library has its own special goals and serves a particular function in its community. A program for young adults can help the library achieve a number of these goals. It can also open up new avenues of service to the community at large and to young people specifically. Library programs can attract new users to the library, increase awareness of the resources and services provided by the library for young adults, help the library become a center of learning, culture, and information in the community, and help the library become a focal point for coordinating the community's resources in areas related to youth. The public library is one of the few places accessible to all members of the community. It serves no special interests, but belongs to all citizens. It is an ideal place for young people with many different attitudes and ideas to come together for discussion. The public library has traditionally served as a center for adult education and has supported the educational and recreational needs of youth. It is a resource center for the community, where people of all ages expect to find all kinds of information. What better agency is there to provide programs where people can explore the human experience through open discussion of the problems and issues facing them and their community?

What if you've tried presenting programs in the library and no one showed up? Does that mean that the young people in your community are not interested in library programs? Not necessarily. Perhaps they were not interested in the particular topic you selected. Maybe they didn't know about the program. Perhaps the timing wasn't right and everyone was involved in another activity. Many things could have gone wrong, so it isn't fair to assume that the young people in your community don't need or aren't interested in library programs. The steps discussed in this section of the book will help you avoid wasting time setting out on the path beloved of the wild goose.

A Word to the Small Library

If you work in a small library and think that the information in this book is directed toward library programming efforts that are too ambitious for smaller libraries, that is not necessarily the case. Even though your budget may be small, programs do not have to cost money. Funds are also available from state-based humanities councils to help libraries present humanities programming. Community volunteers can ease the pressures on an overburdened or small staff. In-kind donations such as volunteer time, meeting room space, and office supplies can help alleviate the problems of matching funds for grants while humanities funding pays for other program costs.

It is wise to keep your programming efforts small until you can build interest in library programs with your intended audience, as well as develop staff support and expertise. You might begin your programming with a film followed by a group discussion. Or you can cosponsor a project in which another group with greater resources does most of the work.

The Uniqueness of Humanities Programs

How does a humanities program differ from a traditional library program? Introducing you to the National Endowment for the Humanities may be the most direct way to answer this question as well as others.

NEH is a government agency that helps scholars, teachers, researchers, librarians, and others demonstrate that the humanities are sources of insight into human problems and priorities and that helps share these insights with the general public. NEH was created in 1965 by a Congress concerned that the realm of ideas keep pace with advancements in science and technology. Congress recognized that careful cultivation of the arts and the humanities was critically important to the development of our nation, and it founded NEH to provide financial support to individuals and institutions, including libraries, through a wide variety of programs. The Endowment supports work in the humanities through programs administered by five divisions—Education Programs, Fellowships and Seminars, General Programs, Research Programs, and State Programs—and by two offices—the Office of Challenge Grants and the Office of Preservation. Within the Division of General Programs is the Humanities Projects in Libraries and Archives section.

The purpose of the Division of General Programs is to foster public understanding and appreciation of the humanities by supporting projects that bring the significant insights of the humanities to general audiences through interpretive exhibitions, lectures, symposia, reading and discussion groups, radio and television programs, printed materials, and other formats. The essence of these projects is the collaboration between scholars in the humanities and individuals (like librarians) with programming experience. This collaboration should reflect the knowledge of the scholars and the expertise of those experienced in public programming. Scholars ensure that the projects include the critical and reflective work of the humanities, while librarians, educators, and other professionals translate the work of scholarship into effective, stimulating, and appealing programs.

Projects supported by NEH's Humanities Projects in Libraries and Archives must focus on ideas and themes central to the disciplines of the humanities. The humanities have to do with humans. They include those branches of learning that deal with the way human beings have felt and behaved and believed with respect to what they consider important or valuable. The humanities are different from the arts, which focus on the products of man's creative skills, and from the sciences, which concentrate on describing and measuring man's physical self and environment.

The humanities include such subjects as philosophy, literature, history, and religion, as well as those aspects of other disciplines that focus on what it means to be human and to make choices and value judgments. In 1965, Congress provided this definition of the humanities:

> The term *humanities* includes, but is not limited to, the study of the following disciplines: history, philosophy, languages, linguistics, literature, archaeology, jurisprudence, the history, theory and criticism of the arts, ethics, comparative religion; and those aspects of the social sciences that employ historical or philosophical approaches.

The important thing to remember is that the humanities have as their central concern the meaning and purpose of human life and relationships. They focus on such questions as the nature of justice, the value of human life and freedom, the relationship between people and the state, and the moral consequences of human action. Such questions form the core of the problems and issues facing everyone, including young people, in your community right now.

A traditional library (or other similar) program becomes a *humanities program* when the disciplines of the humanities are used to explore the subject under consideration. In addition, for the purpose of humanities programs in libraries, librarians serve as the catalysts who bring together the scholar and the public.

The Humanities, Young Adults, and Libraries

The National Endowment for the Humanities, along with state-based humanities councils and other organizations, hopes to foster in the nation's youth an increased awareness of the nature and perspectives of the humanities. By taking part in special projects in history, literature, classics, archaeology, history and criticism of the arts, or other disciplines of the humanities, young people can learn the importance of studying their own culture and heritage and can come to a greater understanding of other cultures as well. They can also develop essential skills of critical inquiry and interpretation that will serve them throughout their lives.

Although students may build a foundation in the humanities in elementary and secondary school, the Endowment encourages other institutions such as libraries to design out-of-school projects for young people. Education can and should continue outside traditional institutions of learning and outside formal schooling. Introducing young people, in their formative years, to the range of institutions, resources, and activities in the humanities that are available to them, outside of school, may encourage a lifelong interest in the humanities and in learning itself. Opportunities to learn throughout life are offered by the nation's libraries, museums, historical organizations, and community centers, as well as by its community colleges, colleges, and universities. Through out-of-school programs, young adults may also be exposed to material and experiences not readily available in the classroom. They may learn to use primary sources and documents available in libraries and archives or to do research using the collections of a museum. Young adults may participate in projects that deal with topics and approaches not usually taught in the schools and may be motivated to pursue additional studies in these areas as part of their formal education.

Humanities programs for young adults should be exciting, challenging, and enticing. They should be clearly focused on specific topics or issues in the disciplines of the humanities. The programs should be designed specifically for a young adult audience, youth of junior or senior high school age. They should take place outside of regular school hours and differ from the regular school curriculum. They must include the participation of scholars with professional training and experience in the disciplines of the humanities addressed by the projects and the participation of persons, like librarians, experienced in programming for young people. Humanities programs should actively involve youth in activities that permit them to learn and apply new knowledge and skills in the humanities.

Humanities Scholars

A scholar in the humanities is someone who is involved in teaching or research, usually in a postsecondary academic setting, in one of the disciplines of the humanities. A scholar may also be someone whose life is devoted to the study and application of the humanities. NEH recognizes, for funding purposes, teachers and scholars who have been trained and professionally involved in one or more of the humanities disciplines and who have a terminal degree (that is, a master's or doctorate) in a humanities discipline.

Scholars in the humanities have been trained to use critical thinking to analyze problems. While they are not magicians or sorcerers who can pull answers out of a hat, they can help us examine the values underlying our actions and decisions and place them in a larger historical and philosophical context. A good definition of what a humanities scholar can do has been offered by the North Dakota Committee for the Humanities and Public Policy:

> Most scholars are gadflies, provokers of discussion, stimulators of reasoning. They do not often see issues in black/white terms; after all, they are professional explorers of the gray area. They: compare the past with the present, ask the right questions, demonstrate that the "right" action depends upon value, show the importance of some things that have no practical value, point out the need for making decisions based on value judgment. Certainly the most important problems deserve this consideration.

You will be using scholars in the humanities in both planning and implementing your program. They will work with you in developing ways in which your program themes can be related to the humanities. Finding the right scholar(s) to help you plan and implement your program is critical. First, you will need a scholar with background in the specific discipline of your project. Second, and most important, that scholar will have to be able to relate to a nonacademic audience, in this case, teenagers. A good source for scholars who have the credentials and the charisma for public programs is the state-based committee or council on the humanities. There is a humanities council in each state, and it usually has information on scholars who are interested in or have had experience in public programming. Local colleges and universities are also excellent resources for humanities scholars. Asking friends and faculty members for recommendations should point you in the right direction.

A successful program will require that you and your scholar work as a team. You are probably more familiar than the scholar with the needs and interests of the young people in your community; and you are aware of the type of programs that will be suitable from the library's standpoint. The scholar can provide subject expertise, as well as the best ways to foster discussion on a pertinent issue. The scholar will also help direct the discussion and raise important questions during the actual program. Select the scholar carefully. Arrange for a face-to-face meeting where you can discuss your ideas and plans. Try to observe the scholar in a classroom situation so you can get an idea about the scholar's speaking style and comfort level in front of an audience. If you feel that the scholar will not be able to relate to or understand a young adult audience, or if you foresee difficulties in working together with the scholar, you have not found the right person. There are many scholars who are eager to work on public humanities programs and who will be valuable assets to your projects. Don't settle for anything less.

How Programs Become Humanities Programs

Young adult librarians have traditionally viewed their role as one that encourages young people to read and love books. To do this, they have used many techniques—booktalks, film festivals, young adult advisory committees, and a variety of informational, educational, and recreational programs. Librarians have developed these techniques and programs to actively involve young people as participants rather than passive observers. In the past, the young adult librarian's goal was the reading of good books that help shape young people's thinking (for example, the classics). In recent years, this emphasis has changed to a more immediate focus on books that are both popular and topical. With the development of humanities programming, the young adult librarian can begin to recapture the tradition and encourage the reading, understanding, and relevance of the classics, as well as more contemporary material.

The young often believe that everything they feel, think, and experience is brand new and unique. They often do not realize that their peers share the same hopes and fears. They cannot imagine that their parents and grandparents faced similar challenges; and the thought that people throughout history have often faced moral and ethical decisions similar to those facing them is often unthinkable. Humanities programs deal with these very issues. Just how different is a teenager's life today from that of life in her grandparents' time? Do modern teenagers really have a different set of ethics than teenagers in the nineteenth century? Or do the values of teenagers today simply masquerade under different clothing and hair styles, more similar than different to those of past generations?

Humanities programs are, then, regular library programs presented from the perspective of the humanities. The actual projects that libraries might develop are limited only by the creativity of the local librarians, the assistance of scholars, and the library's and community's humanities resources. For example, a project might introduce the study of literature and history through the reading and discussion of short stories, novels, poetry, and biography concentrating on a particular theme, such as coming of age. This is a very effective way to relate one's personal experience with adolescence to a universal experience. As young people read and study a particular work, they take a path that allows them to wonder, to question, to compare, to understand. Are things really different now, or is the experience of adolescence the same as it was 40, 50, or 200 years ago? Reading and discussion programs led by humanities scholars are excellent formats for promoting thinking and discussion of such important subjects. The library might enhance the programs with published booklists and book reviews for distribution in the library and in the schools.

Another approach might combine the study of historical events or periods with the reading of historical or biographical works. A historian's interpretation of World War I or II or the Depression, coupled with personal reminiscences as portrayed in biography or autobiography, as well as interaction with people who have lived through these historical periods, might stimulate a young person to consider the impact of current political and societal events on his own life. In conjunction with this program, the library might have some young people, working with scholars, design exhibits and present programs about recent events and the effect they have had on young people today.

The study of philosophy and ethics would also prove a fruitful excursion for young people. How is one's philosophy of life formed? Do we adopt the philosophy of our parents, our teachers, our peers? Are the works of the great philosophers relevant to teenagers? The possibilities are limitless.

3 ♦ "Courtly Love in the Shopping Mall": A Demonstration Program

 reating a good humanities program is almost always a matter of interaction between you and those with general and specific knowledge in the field(s) of interest to your project.

Ideas for good programs come to us in all sorts of unexpected ways. Developing the ideas into workable programs almost certainly means that you will be consulting with a scholar—or for the development of ambitious or complex ideas, with many scholars. In some cases, you might find it advantageous to have a scholar formalize her thinking by fixing it in written form; generally, however, one or more face-to-face meetings with possible follow-ups through phone calls or letters will set you on the right track and keep you there.

What we have done in this book is to ask three scholars—Brenda Murphy, Gregory Stevens, and Michael Bell—to set down their thoughts *from a humanities perspective* on a subject or theme. We took the resulting essays—each one, by the way, written for a different audience—and asked each scholar to get the programming ball rolling by posing some provocative questions that might stimulate discussions among young people.

Using such essays is only one of myriad ways to start the process of humanities programming. We have selected the essay format simply because it is the easiest to replicate in book form. By having the scholars respond in writing, we are not implying that the only way to proceed with the development of a program idea is to have a scholar write a formal essay. Rather, we want to give a sense of contact with the scholar—of how he begins to weigh and shape an idea so that it can be turned into a humanities program. The emphasis is on the collaboration between scholars, librarians, and others interested in creating good humanities programs. Whether it results in a product, like a printed essay, or a process, like a conversation, the sample programs, including the written material by our scholars, are *points of departure for your own humanities programs.*

The three demonstration programs included here were originally created for the YASD/NEH training program that resulted in this book. Each essay, every topic that is sketched out for a possible program, the bibliographic lists—all represent in printed form the process and spirit of collaboration that is the essence of humanities programming. Following each essay is a number of ideas for programs developed from a theme or topic related to the essay, as well as questions that help provoke more thought, both in shaping the program and in participant discussion. Reading and film lists are offered as program resources.

Brenda Murphy's essay, and how she came to write it, provide an excellent preview of what humanities programming for young adults is all about. After you read her account of how the essay and programming ideas evolved, we will take you to a chapter on how to plan humanities programs for young adults. Chapters 7 and 8 contain two more demonstration programs we think you will benefit from examining.

Development of the Theme Material

The essay "Courtly Love in the Shopping Mall" came directly from a stimulating session in which librarians and scholars worked together to develop a humanities program for young adults. Like any such group, this one had to come to a shared understanding of important concepts like *young adult* and *humanities program* before it could begin to address the development of a program. The scholars needed to be enlightened about the accepted library definition of *young adult* and the developmental and social needs that would have to be addressed in any program for this age group, as well as what was possible in library-based programs. The librarians, in turn, needed a clear understanding of the term *humanities* and the definition of *scholar*. In the course of our discussion, the group found that standard definitions of the humanities, such as lists of humanities disciplines or vague generalizations about addressing "the great questions," were not sufficient. This group needed a shared understanding that could be arrived at only through the unique experience of this group of people.

After several hours, the group's touchstone experience happened. A librarian who was frustrated by the vagueness of the definitions put the problem squarely. She had plenty of ideas for programs. What she needed to know was whether they had "humanities content." What exactly was the required content of a humanities program? At this, an equally frustrated historian responded that it was not the content or subject that made for a program in the humanities, but the questions that were asked about it. Pointing to a clock on the wall, he said that the clock could be the subject of a fine humanities program because it suggested a number of questions about human values, experience, and civilization. As a historian, he wondered about the clock's role in the development of civilization. When and why did the clock come into use? What cultural and social needs demanded the measurement of time? How have those needs changed, and how has the development of the clock responded to those needs? Why has it become necessary to measure time more and more precisely?

At this point, the folklorist in the group suggested a whole new set of questions. As an object, the clock raised aesthetic issues. Was it produced primarily for beauty or for utility—in other words, was it a work of art or an artifact? Was its producer an artist? What role did the clock as an object play in its culture? How was the style of the clock related to the prevailing concept of time? Was it circular, suggesting that time was a cycle connected with nature, or was it digital, suggesting that time existed in fixed, isolated moments? Did the clock measure seconds or just minutes? Did it have numbers, suggesting that precise measurement was important, or was its face blank, suggesting that design was its maker's primary concern?

With this exchange as a base, the group proceeded to an exciting discussion not only about clocks and time, but about using humanities questions as the focus for programs for young adults. As the collaboration between librarians and scholars developed, the touchstone experience of the clock was always there as a reminder of the group's central focus on the humanities. It was only because the group had gone through an experience of discovering a common definition of the humanities that it was able to function effectively as a group.

After its first session on fundamentals, the group was ready to go on to the question of specific humanities programs. Because we now shared basic assumptions about important humanities questions, it was relatively easy to generate in a short brainstorming session a random list of possible topics for young adults. Analyzing the list, a librarian found that the topics fell naturally into three areas, which she called: "Recycled Lives: Who Went Before Me?"; "Finding the Center: Who Am I Now?"; and "Future Tensions: Where Am I Going?"

After the initial stage of collaboration, the scholars tried to develop a conceptual idea and humanities questions for a program based on one of the topics, while the librarians worked to create program ideas and materials. After fixing on "Courtly Love in the Shopping Mall" as a promising topic, I listed the humanities disciplines that I thought would raise interesting questions about love, courtship, music and dance, and fashion for young adults. Among the possibilities were cultural and social history, literature, philosophy, art history, folklore, and the history of dance.

Thinking about the courtly love topic from the perspectives of various disciplines, I raised questions that might be of interest to young adults. Love and courtship suggested such questions as: What is courtly love? How did the idea arise? How did the medieval and renaissance people conceive of love, marriage, and courtship? What was a love relationship to them? How does the notion of courtly love differ from contemporary notions of a love relationship? What aspects of courtship are universal, and what aspects are rooted in a particular place and time, and why? What social, moral, and cultural values are being expressed through different courtship customs at different times and in different places?

The idea of fashion as courtship suggested questions like: How have fashions changed through history? Why did people in various places and at various times dress as they did? What aspect of the human body is emphasized by a particular fashion? What does this tell us about the wearer's conception of beauty, as well as things like climate, class, and occupation? What role do clothes play in courtship? What are the fashions for young adults now? What does the choice of a style tell about a person in the youth culture? What kinds of judgments are made about others based on their choice of style?

The next step after defining the humanities questions for ourselves was writing an essay that would be used as part of a library program and that would pose these questions to young adults. The essay that follows was written to introduce the program to the young adult participants and to suggest the questions they might want to explore throughout the program's various activities.

Courtly Love in the Shopping Mall

by Brenda Murphy

Courtly love, or *amour courtois,* is a concept that came out of the songs of the troubadours who entertained the courts of kings and noblemen in the later Middle Ages. The term, which really means "courteous love," was part of an attempt to civilize the knights, who often behaved more like a modern motorcycle gang than like the "knights in shining armor" familiar to us from popular books, songs, and movies about the medieval period. Through the singers and poets of that time, a very elaborate code for courtly love developed, and it was seen as the ideal for centuries to come.

Courtly love was the "love from afar" that a knight had for a lady. He thought of her as more virtuous than he, and his whole object in life was to do enough brave deeds to be worthy of her love. This is where the idea of climbing the highest mountain, swimming the deepest river, and crossing the widest desert as expressions of love came

Brenda Murphy is a professor of English at the University of Connecticut at Storrs.

from. The lover was supposed to be ennobled by the suffering he went through for his lady, and only then would he become worthy of her. This often took as long as twenty years, during which the lover was often so overcome by the depth of his passion that he became pale and melancholy, lost his appetite, and trembled, sighed, or wept at a moment's notice. The lover would often express his love through songs and poems that he would send to his lady anonymously. He would also try to win her favor by behaving courteously, which meant paying a lot of attention to his clothing and appearance, as well as knowing how to dance and how to talk about something besides hunting and fighting.

There are a lot of differences between these lovers and today's, of course. In the 1990s, most girls don't sit around waiting for someone to fall in love with them, and most boys don't tremble, sigh, and weep as signs that they like a girl. The rules of the game have changed, but we still do a lot of the things the courtly lovers did, in slightly different ways. Every culture has its courtship customs, which are really just ways of getting to know people of the opposite sex and getting them to like us. Rock music and contemporary dances may seem very different from the songs of the troubadours and the intricate dances of the Middle Ages, but they perform the same functions. The songs express love, passion, and the unique feelings of a young generation. Dances provide a way for young people to meet and enjoy their music together, as well as to enjoy each other's attractions.

Now what does all of this have to do with shopping malls? The clothes you put on to wear to the mall where you see your friends are a contemporary version of the courtly lover's velvet doublet and silk hose. In the past, the king's court, the town square, the general store, and the malt shop have been sites where boys and girls could meet— and court. In many ways, the shopping mall is where the contemporary version of courtly love takes place.

The Customs of Courtship

Looking at courtship customs from other times and places can help us understand what is going on in our own lives. It can give us a new vantage point for looking at our own customs by helping us see what is unique to us and what seems to be part of being young in all times and places. Some courtship customs sound peculiar from our point of view. During the eighteenth century, for example, it was common for a young couple in the New England colonies to get to know each other by "bundling." They would lie side by side on a bed, each wrapped up in a quilt, with a board down the middle of the bed as a barrier between them.

This may sound like a strange way to spend a Sunday afternoon, but if you consider the context, it makes sense. Most of these people were farmers who had large families and only one heated room downstairs where the whole family would gather on a Sunday. They were religious people who did not think it was proper for young people to go off by themselves, but they were also sensitive to the need for people to get to know each other before they decided to marry. Because the only place available was the one unheated bedroom, the solution was to give the room to the young couple, but to make the boundaries between them clear. Because most people in our culture don't share these eighteenth-century social and religious views or the limitations on space, privacy, and heat, this custom no longer suits our needs, so it seems odd to us.

A custom that seems universal can also have very different meanings in different times and places, as Nicolas Perella has shown in *The Kiss Sacred and Profane*. To the early Mexicans and the Phoenicians, a kiss was a powerful religious symbol that signified the joining of life forces, or souls. As late as 1897, the Chinese, who had no custom of kissing on the lips, were horrified when they saw Westerners do it. In the code of courtly love, a single kiss was the sign that the lady accepted the lifetime devotion of her courtly lover. In the Victorian era (1850 to 1900), a middle-class American girl allowed herself to be kissed by a boy for the first time only when they became engaged, and if she allowed it before then, her purity was considered compromised and she would lose her status as a potential bride. The Victorians also had a double standard. Boys were allowed much more freedom than girls, and a boy might "ruin" several girls without affecting his own good social standing. During the roaring twenties, the custom of "necking" came in along with the automobile, and kissing became one of the signs of youthful rebellion. Young couples who necked openly were considered daring and "fast." In the forties and fifties, the good night kiss was a ritual. A good girl allowed one kiss per date as a sign of affection. More than that might be considered necking, and the girl might be considered "easy," a modern version of the Victorian "compromised."

These differences express underlying social, cultural, and moral values, and understanding these differences helps us clarify our own values and compare them with those of other times and places. Understanding the values underlying different customs can help us understand why some customs are common to nearly every group of people, while others are limited to a specific place and time.

Music and Dance

In some ways, we owe rock music to the troubadours. It was the court singers and poets who put music and dance at the center of our expression of love and passion. As one twelfth-century troubadour sang:

> A song cannot in any way have value
> If the singing doesn't spring from heart,
> And the singing cannot well from breast
> Unless its source is fine, true love.

And so my verse looms high,
For I have joy from love, devoting there
My mouth and eyes, my heart and mind.

Medieval Song: An Anthology of Hymns and Lyrics,
translated by James J. Wilhelm

What has happened in the 800 years since this troubadour wrote his love songs? The history of popular music shows that the concerns of love and youth have been central themes ever since, though, of course, the view of love and the way people in love express it have changed. Descriptions of how the lover is overcome by golden hair, teeth like pearls, lips like cherries, and skin like lilies have given way to more direct expressions of passion.

Perhaps because popular music and dance have been the expressions of youth, they have often been seen as rebellious activities. It seems incredible that in our time the waltz was condemned as indecent and dangerous because young people were bound to lose control of themselves if they held each other so closely. During the fifties, rock and roll was seen as a threat to teenage morality. When Elvis Presley appeared on the "Ed Sullivan Show," he could be filmed only from the waist up because his dancing was thought too suggestive for a teenage audience. In 1956, the host of a popular show called "Juke Box Jury" voiced a widespread popular opinion when he said that all rhythm and blues records were dirty and as bad for kids as dope.

Even the most recent history shows the constant struggle between the younger generation's desire for self-expression and the older generation's concern that love songs not be too explicit. In 1985, the Parents' Music Resource Center persuaded the record industry to put advisories on album and cassette covers identifying recordings that are believed to contain sexually explicit language.

Looking at music and dance in different times and places, we can begin to sort out what is bound to a particular culture and what is universal. The waltz certainly looks to us like the most innocent of dances, and in the early 1960s, when couples began to separate on the dance floor and do their own versions of the twist and the jerk, the older generation complained that they were dancing too far apart. Compared to contemporary bands, Elvis Presley, Chuck Berry, and the Beatles seem tame, even quaint, and young people wonder what the fuss was back then.

How much of the objection to the waltz or to rock and roll was a response to that specific dance or music, and how much was just the natural response of older people to younger people who want things different from the way the older generation likes them? Is there a natural connection among youth, love, sex, and rebellion? How have the attitudes expressed toward love and toward relationships in popular song lyrics changed? Does the changing style of music and dance reflect cultural, historical, and political changes as they happen? As we consider these questions in relation to other cultures and attitudes, we can begin to understand our own much better.

Fashion
Courtly lovers popularized the idea of dressing to attract the opposite sex, but fashion has always existed as a way of emphasizing the beauty of the human form. Looking at the clothes they consider attractive can give us a good sense of what the people in a given time and place consider beautiful. The loose drapery of the classical Greeks emphasized the soft curves of the body, while the Romans favored shorter tunics that exposed muscular arms and legs. During the early Middle Ages, Europeans wore long, shapeless robes that covered them from head to toe, deemphasizing the body. Some historians have seen this fashion as evidence of the medieval concern with spiritual values rather than material things.

Later, when courtly love was in full flower, European men began to wear short coats, or doublets, and hose-like tights, emphasizing their legs, while women wore dresses with low necklines and tightly drawn-in waistlines, emphasizing their breasts and hips. During the last 700 years, a great many fads have reflected the passing notions of beauty and emphasis of various parts of the body. In the fourteenth century, pregnant Dutch women tried to make their stomachs as prominent as possible, with full dresses gathered in the front, and Victorian women wore padded bustles that stuck out in the rear. In the seventeenth century, aristocratic European men wore shoulder-length curled and powdered hair, embroidered silk waistcoats, and big hats with enormous feathers, emphasizing the value they placed on displaying their wealth and freedom from physical labor. In the mid-nineteenth century, American women wore crinolines, with waists held in so tightly by whalebone corsets that many of the women developed problems with breathing and blood circulation. Their five-foot-wide hoop skirts made it impossible to sit down and sometimes to get through doors, but they made the women appear tiny and delicate, which was considered essential to female beauty at the time.

During the twentieth century, American women have moved away from the ideal of the hourglass figure toward thinner and thinner lines, and in the last two decades, there has been more emphasis on muscle tone for both women and men. Many commentators see this as a move toward androgyny, a breakdown of the differences in the ideal conception of the male and female forms. Is this true today? What aspects of the male and female forms do current fashions emphasize? How do current fashions dictate our own ideals of beauty? Do we sacrifice comfort and practicality to these ideals? How do we use clothes to attract other people? There is much that our choice of clothing can tell us about ourselves and our values.

Fashion has also been a reflection of social and political values throughout history. The change at the beginning of the nineteenth century from impractical knee breeches and stockings for gentlemen to the long pants that were originally worn only by laborers was part of a general movement toward breaking down class differences after the French Revolution. During the 1960s, a similar movement took place when the great majority of young Americans abandoned ties and dresses and started wearing the blue jeans that had been the clothing of the working man. What social values are reflected now in the choice of a certain style of dress? Preppy, jock, greaser, punk—what social or political statement are you making with your clothes? What is the source of attraction or repulsion you feel when you are confronted with a certain style of dress, even before you talk to the person? What effect does this have on who you meet and how you get to know someone?

Looking closely at the clothes we see in the local mall can teach us a great deal, not only about our own culture's ideal of beauty, but about our sense of ourselves and the values we use in judging others.

Spreading Paint

If you think of library humanities programming as a kind of magical paint with which we can dress the surface of things so that surface sheds light and color, then we could say that discussion is one of the basic vehicles for the pigment the scholar provides us. Most humanities programs, in large or minor measure, involve the use of discussion groups, question and answer, and verbal presentations with audience involvement.

It has long been demonstrated that much of human learning results from verbal interaction like the types described above. To give you a firsthand feeling for programming, each of the sample programs following will include a discussion of the essay as an example of how the scholars involved with YA programming might provoke thought and discussion.

Overall Theme to Be Explored

Brenda Murphy's essay looks at patterns of courtship from the Middle Ages to the twentieth century. The ways that men and women meet and indicate their interest in each other have always been governed by various codes of behavior. These codes have adapted to the economic and social conditions of specific historical periods. Explorations of these rituals can give insight into the philosophy and meaning of the relationships between the sexes and into the broader implications for society as a whole. The rituals and manners of love and romance are the subject of this theme unit.

Using the essay, you can now generate ideas for library YA programs. We have selected some possible program topics for this sample unit, using the following humanities disciplines: history; literature; history of art or architecture; history of music; philosophy. You can approach these disciplines using the following questions:

> How have courtship rituals changed over the centuries?
>
> What purpose do these rituals serve?
>
> How is the course of love affected by the clothes we wear? The music we listen to?
>
> Has the language of love changed? If so, how?
>
> What roles do love and romance play in marriage in the Middle Ages? In Victorian times? Today?
>
> How are courtship customs affected by the economic condition of a particular era?
>
> How have the relations between the sexes changed since the nineteenth century? What impact has this had on courting customs?

Programs by Topic

With these questions in mind, we can now start sketching some programs by topics such as "Courtship Customs," "Fashion," "Music and Dance in Courtship," and "Love and Romance." Below we have suggested some possible programs using a particular topic as a focal point. We have offered ideas for program formats, along with a perspective of the topics from the humanities point of view. Following the suggested topics, the last section of the unit provides a resource list of books and films that might be used in programming.

TOPIC: Courtship Customs I

One important aspect of courtship is the opportunity for young people to meet. Though the place has changed through the ages, certain types of public buildings have provided natural courting places.

Program Title: "The Courting Place: The Village Square to the Shopping Mall."

Format: Slide/lecture.

Humanities Focus: Ask an architectural historian to give a slide show and lecture that demonstrate how architecture has facilitated or limited contact between the sexes. Relate this to social attitudes of the time with the help of a social historian; contrast it with today's shopping mall design and current social attitudes.

Scholar's Questions and Comments: Prompt discussion of the early courts, plazas, squares, and malls that explains how each place encourages interaction. Why were these places effective? What characteristics encouraged young people to meet? Why were they socially acceptable? How does the architecture of the mall encourage or limit social contact?

YA Involvement: The young adult participants could be asked to share the reasons they go to the mall and comment on their views of social interaction there. The participants could also compare malls in the area and comment on the function of their various designs. Do they move people through and really focus on the stores, or do they encourage congregating? Are they purely mercantile establishments, or do they try to function as the forum of the community through programming activities?

In a small town, YAs could also identify local congregating places such as the post office, barber shop, feed store, parking lots, parks, and so on and discuss the reasons why these became meeting places and the particular groups that they serve.

Promotion: The program could be advertised in the local mall.

Films: American Graffiti; Fast Times at Ridgemont High.

TOPIC: Courtship Customs II

Program Title: "The Romantic Quest, or How Can I Impress Her/Him?"

Format 1: A reading discussion series based on medieval love poetry, classics, and current YA novels that demonstrate the lover performing a heroic feat to impress the beloved.

Format 2: A readers' theater presentation using the same kind of material in Format 1.

Humanities Focus: The readings will be used to show how lovers in different historical periods sought to attract the attention of the opposite sex. The language of the poetry and the novels could also be used to demonstrate romantic concepts.

Scholar's Questions and Comments: Define *masculine*. Define *feminine*. What are your expectations of each role? Are there characteristics that are specific to each sex? Have these roles changed over the centuries? Is it always the boy's role to impress the girl, or did girls reverse this role in the 1980s? What was a romantic quest in the Middle Ages? Do romantic quests still exist? What is the modern equivalent of a courtly love poem?

Books and Films: Little Women; Daisy Miller; The Importance of Being Earnest; Pride and Prejudice; The Love Poems of John Donne.

Topic: Courtship Customs III

One program could explore the manners and conventions that guided lovers, past and present.

Program Title: "The Art of Flirting, Then and Now."

Format: A film or video series of works that demonstrates past manners, courtly language, and flirtation.

Humanities Focus: Using clips of romantic scenes, the scholar can demonstrate how conversation, accessories (flowers, fans, etc.), and manners were used to indicate attraction and can show similarities and differences. The demonstration would also show how certain values or qualities (beauty, courage, and devotion, for example) were expressed by flirting.

Scholar's Questions and Comments: What methods did men and women use to flirt in the Middle Ages? In the Victorian period? Today? What purpose does/did flirting serve? Are/were customs different among different economic classes? In the past, were certain gifts more romantic than others? Are those same gifts popular today? Is flirting an artificial act, or does it express a deeper significance?

YA Involvement: A panel of YAs could react to scholars' comments, discussing present dating etiquette and language. They might respond to the question, "Do young people today flirt?" YAs could do improvisations representing contemporary flirtation.

Films and Videos: Tom Jones; Ivanhoe; Pride and Prejudice; Camelot; Jezebel; A Streetcar Named Desire; Saturday Night Fever.

Topic: Fashion

Program Title: "What to Wear to the Mall."

Format: An exhibit of pictures, fashion magazines, and clothes and accessories or a fashion show using teenagers followed by a panel discussion. Panelists might include an art historian, a psychologist, and a local fashion personality.

Humanities Focus: By exploring the clothes worn by young people during different historical eras, the scholars and the audience can discuss how fashion changes reflect societal changes.

Scholar's Questions and Comments: What constitutes attraction between the sexes? Can fashion be viewed as a social or political indicator? Have turbulent historical periods produced revolutionary dress styles? What is beautiful? Why are certain body types more popular in one era than another (hourglass figure versus the flapper)? Who sets fashion trends? Do the young dress like the older leaders or set their own styles? Was this always true?

YA Involvement: YAs could help with the research and production of the exhibit or fashion show.

Books: Alison Lurie, *The Language of Clothes*; Valerie Steele, *Fashion and Eroticism: Ideals of Feminine Beauty from the Victorian Era to the Jazz Age.*

TOPIC: Music and Dance in Courtship

Another program could explore how music, song, and dance express the rituals of courtship.

Program Title: "Say It with Music."

Format: A music festival: demonstrations of songs, dances, and music followed by scholars' comments (through a speech, a panel, etc.).

Humanities Focus: The program could provide an overview of romantic musical material, with historians, artists, and scholars of literature looking at the meanings of both the lyrics and the dance movements as courting rituals.

Scholar's Questions and Comments: A new dance is often viewed as threatening whether it is the waltz or the slam. Why? How does dancing encourage the courting ritual? How has dancing changed over the decades? Examine the difference between an Elizabethan song and a modern ballad. Are they saying the same thing? Does each conform to specific literary rules for expression?

YA Involvement: Use YAs as performers, dancers, musicians, and singers.

Promotion: The program could be advertised on the local radio station prospective YA participants listen to.

Book: L. T. Topsfield, *Troubadours and Love.*

TOPIC: Love and Romance

Title: "The Kiss through the Ages."

Format: An exhibit of paintings, prints and memorabilia—such as Victorian valentines—portraying couples kissing and embracing during different time periods. This could be combined with a lecture by a scholar (of history, art history, or literature) to explore the moral, social, and even political significance of a kiss and the broader concepts of love and romance illustrated by the exhibit.

Humanities Focus: This is an opportunity to look at the moral values and societal conventions that form the images representing love, romance, and lust in different eras.

Scholar's Questions and Comments: What is love? What is romance? Is there a difference? Has our concept of love and romance changed over the years? What is sentiment? Are any of the exhibit materials sentimental? Was this typical of certain periods?

Promotion Ideas: Schedule your program for Valentine's Day. Use a variety of romantic symbols in your advertising.

Portrait of a Young Adult Program

The sample programs listed above are intended to be outlines of possible program topics and formats. You could develop these more fully to a next step, a more detailed and elaborate program. The program outlines certainly could be used with a minimum of fuss to start some modest programs at little or no cost.

We offer below an example of a demonstration program you might try in your library. With some assistance from local scholars, you could submit a proposal based on this program for funding to your state-based humanities council or to a similar public or private agency.

Boy Meets Girl: Then and Now

A Sample Program in the Series: Courtly Love in the Shopping Mall

"Boy Meets Girl" is an example of a humanities program for young adults that could be put on in a local library with minimal funding and minimal time. The participants might include a scholar who is a member of the English, theater arts, or speech/communications department at the local college, members of the library staff, and young adults. The readings for the program would be chosen by the participants, with each member of the group contributing his expertise about the literary texts that best express the chosen theme, the texts that would most appeal to a young adult audience, and the suitability of the texts to the readers' theater format and the available cast, made up of volunteers from the young adults and the library staff. Readers' theater can be done for an audience of young adults with or without costumes and staging. A performance of the script of "Boy Meets Girl" requires a minimal stage setting of a table and three chairs.

Goals
> To make young adults more aware of the universality of human experience.
> To help young adults see the social and cultural forces that influence the choices they make about human relationships.
> To give young adults a cultural and historical context in which to understand the nature and conception of love.
> To make young adults aware of the social and cultural codes that dictate their behavior with the opposite sex, and therefore to make young adults freer to make choices about this behavior.

Objectives
> To produce a readers' theater program comparing three literary representations of courtship in Shakespeare's plays with three representations in contemporary literature, including young adult literature.
> To involve an audience of 30 young adults and a literary scholar in a discussion of significant issues in the humanities arising from the readers' theater production.
> To train five young adults, through their participation in the program, in the methods of readers' theater in order to establish a standing advisory group for future readers' theater productions.
> To establish a link with the local college through the identification of a humanities scholar who is eager to participate in public programs with the public library.

Schedule of Readings
> 1. Courtly Love—Readings from William Shakespeare. *Taming of the Shrew:* Act I, scene i, lines 143–75. *The Tempest:* Act III, scene i, lines 15–90. *Much Ado about Nothing:* Act IV, scene i, lines 255–330.
> 2. Contemporary Courtship—Readings from Contemporary Literature. Ntosake Shange, *Betsey Brown:* pages 71–75. Judy Blume, *Forever:* pages 14–18. Christopher Durang, *Beyond Therapy:* Act I, scene i.

Notes for Narrating
The following notes might be used by the scholar who narrates the program and facilitates the discussion. The short introductions set the scene for the readers' theater selections, and the notes on issues serve as suggestions for the issues the scholar might want to bring out during the discussion of the texts. Of course, your local scholar should feel free to add her own comments and interpretations to the introduction and program discussion.

I. Shakespeare

1. Introduction: *Taming of the Shrew*
   Lucentio and his servant Tranio have just witnessed a scene in which old Baptista has refused to allow his beautiful daughter Bianca to marry any of her three suitors until he has disposed of her shrewish sister Kate. Lucentio has fallen in love with Bianca at first sight and stands in a kind of stupor as the scene opens.

Issues for Discussion: What is the attraction of courtly love based on? Does this kind of attraction really exist? If so, how long is it likely to last? What is the ideal that Bianca represents, as Lucentio articulates it? Is it universal, or is it particular to this culture?

2. Introduction: *The Tempest*
   Miranda has grown up with her father on an otherwise deserted island. The only human beings she can remember having seen are her father and their servant, the barely human Caliban. A young prince, Ferdinand, becomes marooned on the island, falls in love with Miranda at first sight, and decides to become a servant to her father in order to be near her. Ferdinand is stacking wood as the scene opens.

Issues for Discussion: Does the attitude of contemporary young people toward relationships differ from that of the characters? If so, how? Why? Is there still an ideal of the kind of undying love Ferdinand professes? Does the assumption still exist that the person one loves is the best person; that is, does virtue equal beauty equal attractiveness? What does our culture consider attractive?

3. Introduction: *Much Ado about Nothing*
   Beatrice's cousin Hero has been betrayed in love by Claudio. As the scene opens, Benedick, who is in love with Beatrice, sees her crying and comes to comfort her.

Issues for Discussion: What do Beatrice and Benedick expect of each other? Is Beatrice's expectation unheard of in the twentieth century, or are there still elements of this in contemporary relationships? What are the expectations that a declaration of love produces? Is there an element of manipulation inherent in the male-female love relationship?

II. Contemporary Courtship

1. Introduction: *Betsey Brown*

At twelve, Betsey, the daughter of a black doctor in St. Louis, is beginning to be interested in boys, particularly a basketball player named Eugene Boyd, but she still likes to do "kid things" like climb trees. She has climbed a tree to forget some trouble at school as the scene opens.

Issues for Discussion: What is the code of sexual decorum to which Betsey holds herself? What does she think Eugene expects of her, and why does she treat him the way she does? Is this unique to Betsey's upbringing, or are these more universal values? Are there deeper cultural values that occasion them? How do cultural codes influence individual behavior today?

2. Introduction: *Forever*

Kathy is staying at her friend Sybil's house. At a party, she meets a boy named Michael, who, like her, is a senior in high school. Even though she is interested in him, she has made a point of avoiding him at the party. The next morning he comes to Sybil's house to pick up his records, and he goes to the basement to pick them out of the stack. A few seconds later, he calls, "Who's K.D.?"

Issues for Discussion: What is the basis for the attraction between Kathy and Michael? Does it differ appreciably from that of the courtly lovers in Shakespeare's plays? How does this contemporary couple relate to each other? Are they equals in this relationship? Who is the more aggressive? Who initiates the sexual contact? Why? What does the exchange about skiing establish in the relationship? Is Kathy playing a role, or is she acting honestly on her feelings? Why does she allow Michael to initiate the relationship and take the role of teacher even though she is older than he is? Is this a realistic reflection of a young adult relationship in the 1980s?

3. Introduction: *Beyond Therapy*

The scene is a New York restaurant. "Bruce is seated, looking at his watch. He is thirty to thirty-four, fairly pleasant-looking, probably wearing a blazer with an open shirt. Enter Prudence, twenty-nine to thirty-two, attractive, semi-dressed up in a dress or nice skirt and blouse. After hesitating a moment, she crosses to Bruce."

Issues for Discussion: What is Durang making fun of? How do the rituals of the 1980s compare with the courtly love rituals of Shakespeare's time? How well does love at first sight translate into commitment at first sight? What expectations do these two have of each other and of a relationship? Is this an accurate reflection of American values in the 1980s?

A Sample Bibliography

The following bibliography on courtship, fashion, and beauty was developed through suggestions from the YASD/NEH Project Advisory Committee. It gives you an idea of the kinds of material you can find for a theme in local library collections. By working with scholars in various humanities disciplines (music, literature, art history, history), support material can be identified that will add to this and other program themes.

Courtship History and Customs

Bailey, Beth. *From Front Porch to Back Seat*. Johns Hopkins Univ. Press, 1988.

Brasch, Rudolph. *How Did It Begin? Customs and Superstitions and Their Romantic Origins*. McKay, 1965.

Campbell, Patricia J. *Sex Education Books for Young Adults 1892–1979*. Bowker, 1979.

Merser, Cheryl. *Honorable Intentions: The Manners of Courtship in the '80s*. Atheneum, 1983.

Rothman, Ellen K. *Hands and Hearts: A History of Courtship in America*. Basic Books, 1984.

Topsfield, L. T. *Troubadours and Love*. Cambridge Univ. Press, 1975.

Turner, E. S. *A History of Courting*. Dutton, 1955.

Fashion and Beauty

Boucher, Francois. *20,000 Years of Fashion: The History of Costume and Personal Adornment*. Abrams, 1967.

Freedman, Rita. *Beauty Bound: Why We Pursue the Myth in the Mirror*. Lexington, 1986.

Lurie, Alison. *The Language of Clothes*. Random, 1981.

Melinkoff, Ellen. *What We Wore: An Offbeat Social History of Women's Clothing, 1950 to 1980*. Quill, 1984.

Steele, Valerie. *Fashion and Eroticism: Ideals of Feminine Beauty from the Victorian Era to the Jazz Age*. Oxford, 1985.

Love in Classics

Austen, Jane. *Pride and Prejudice.* Dodd.

In this witty English novel originally published in 1813, the love between feisty Elizabeth Bennett and proud aristocratic Darcy overcomes their family obstacles and initial prejudices.

Brontë, Charlotte. *Jane Eyre.* Dodd.

Orphaned, poor, and alone, governess Jane is loved by her employer, Mr. Rochester, but his great house hides an agonizing secret. Originally published in 1847.

Brontë, Emily. *Wuthering Heights.* Dodd.

Set against the bleak, windswept moors of northern England, this passionate novel, originally published in 1874, tells how Cathy's betrayal of her love for Heathcliff leads to a bitter cycle of hatred and revenge.

Dreiser, Theodore. *An American Tragedy.* Bentley.

A poor young man gets the chance to win wealth and pleasure, but first he must get rid of the ordinary girl who loves him. Originally published in 1925.

du Maurier, Daphne. *Rebecca.* Doubleday.

Married to a wealthy widower, a shy young woman feels overwhelmed by the memories of her husband's dazzling first wife and the secrets of his great English estate. Originally published in 1938.

Hardy, Thomas. *Tess of the D'Urbervilles.* Merrimack Pub. Circle.

Tess is a victim—first of the rich man who seduces her and then of her intellectual husband, Angel Clare, who cannot forgive her loss of purity. Originally published in 1891.

Hemingway, Ernest. *A Farewell to Arms.* Scribner.

A wounded American ambulance driver falls passionately in love with a Scottish nurse in the muddle and horror of the Italian front during World War I. Originally published in 1929.

La Farge, Oliver. *Laughing Boy.* Houghton.

Set in 1915 in the Navaho country of the Southwest, this is a love story of Slim Girl, who has been corrupted by white values, and Laughing Boy, who knows nothing of the whites. First published in 1929.

Lawrence, D. H. *Sons and Lovers.* Penguin.

Paul Morel's deep bond with his mother complicates his love for sensitive young Miriam and for passionate older Clara. Originally published in 1913.

Maugham, W. Somerset. *Of Human Bondage.* Doubleday.

Orphaned, talented Philip Carey, disabled with a clubfoot, becomes obsessed with a shallow young woman until he breaks free to find work and true love. Originally published in 1915.

Mitchell, Margaret. *Gone with the Wind.* Macmillan.

The relationship between ruthless, passionate Scarlett O'Hara and blockade-runner Rhett Butler is set against the turmoil of the Civil War. Originally published in 1936.

Tolstoy, Leo. *Anna Karenina.* Penguin.

Anna tragically destroys her life when she falls passionately in love with Count Vronsky and leaves her narrow husband, who then denies her access to her beloved child. Originally published in 1877.

Undset, Sigrid. *Kristin Lavransdatter.* Knopf.

A realistic, richly characterized trilogy set in Norway during the fourteenth century tells of Kristin's childhood and her experiences as lover, wife, and mother. Originally published in 1922.

Love in Poetry

All for Love. Ed. and illus. by Tasha Tudor. Putnam/Philomel, 1984.

A romantic, sometimes sentimental, collection of letters, poems, and songs in an illustrated, large-size format.

A Book of Love Poetry. Ed. by Jon Stallworthy. Oxford, 1974.

Two thousand years of love poetry, some in translation, arranged by theme from young love to maturity.

Browning, Elizabeth Barrett. *Sonnets from the Portuguese and Other Love Poems.* Doubleday.

A series of love poems, first published in 1850, written for her poet-husband, Robert Browning, with whom she ran away from her tyrannical Victorian father.

Donne, John. *The Love Poems of John Donne.* Ed. by Charles Fawkes. St. Martin's, 1982.

Love poems from the seventeenth century that are witty, irreverent, passionate, and philosophical.

Love Is Like the Lion's Tooth: An Anthology of Love Poems. Ed. by Frances McCullough. Harper, 1984.

Passion, not romance, is the theme of this fine, small, teenage anthology (much in translation) that expresses the intensity of love's various moods and stages.

Rock Voices: The Best Lyrics of an Era. Ed. with text by Matt Damsker. St. Martin's, 1980.

A collection (with commentary) of 49 rock songs from the 1960s and 1970s, including selections by such writers as Bob Dylan, Paul Simon, the Beatles, and Bruce Springsteen.

Tennyson, Alfred Lord. *The Lady of Shalott*. Illus. by Charles Keeping. Oxford, 1986.

Keeping's stormily romantic black-and-white drawings illustrate the famous poem of the lonely lady, cursed to remain in her castle, whose love for the dazzling knight Sir Lancelot makes her break free and die.

Love in Fantasy

Finney, Jack. *Time and Again*. Simon & Schuster, 1970.

As part of a top-secret government project, Simon Morley steps back in time to the New York City of the 1880s, where he meets and falls in love with Julia.

Le Guin, Ursela K. *The Beginning Place*. Harper, 1980.

Hugh and Irena are brought together by their responsibility to save the magic world beyond the "beginning place" in a story that is as much romance as fantasy.

McKinley, Robin. *Beauty: A Retelling of the Story of Beauty and the Beast*. Harper, 1978.

A sensitive, bookish young woman who is not especially pretty saves the beast through the power of her love in a richly characterized, romantic retelling of the fairy tale.

Mahy, Margaret. *The Changeover: A Supernatural Romance*. Atheneum/ Margaret K. McElderry, 1984.

When New Zealand teenager Laura uses her latent supernatural powers to save her beloved younger brother from an evil demon, she is helped by a boy who loves her to change over into her powerful self.

Meaney, Dee Morrison. *Iseult*. Berkley/Ace, 1985.

In a retelling of the passionate Celtic story, Tristan and Iseult become lovers when Tristan is forced to woo her for his beloved king.

Synge, Ursula. *Swan's Wing*. Bodley Head, 1984.

In an atmospheric extension of the Andersen fairy tale *Wild Swans*, Matthew, a moody and tormented sculptor in search of perfection, joins Lothar, a one-winged prince, and falls in love with the goose girl Gerda, who, in turn, loves Lothar.

Wilhelm, Kate. *Oh, Susannah!* Houghton, 1982.

Falling in love with Susannah, a young woman stricken with an involuntary tall-tale-telling syndrome, graduate student Brad joins in the hot pursuit of a strange, roaming blue suitcase that escapes from Susannah.

Willard, Nancy. *Things Invisible to See.* Knopf, 1985.

A baseball batted lightheartedly into a summer evening strikes and paralyzes Clare, and while Ben's guilt makes him visit Clare, their growing love keeps him at her side—and later enables the pair to survive the supernatural machinations of Ben's evil twin.

Falling in Love

Adler, C. S. *Roadside Valentine.* Macmillan, 1983.

Jamie loves Louisa, but she is in love with someone else; so he attracts her attention (and invokes his father's anger) by carving her a roadside valentine made of snow.

Baldwin, James. *If Beale Street Could Talk.* Doubleday/Dial, 1974.

Twenty-year-old Fonny, wrongly imprisoned for rape, and 19-year-old Tish, pregnant with Fonny's child, support each other in their struggle against injustice and racial opression in Harlem.

Blume, Judy. *Forever.* Bradbury, 1975.

Drawn together, in part, by physical magnetism, Katherine and Michael have sex on a regular basis until Kath guiltily realizes she is attracted to someone else.

Bond, Nancy. *A Place to Come Back To.* Atheneum/Margaret K. McElderry, 1984.

An intense but understated story about teenagers Oliver and Charlotte, friends since childhood, who find their relationship changing when Oliver, in a crisis, reaches out for Charlotte's love.

Daly, Maureen. *Seventeenth Summer.* Dodd, 1985.

The summer before she enters college is a telling one for Angie Morrow, who meets Jack Duluth and spends June, July, and August falling in love. This gently told romance, originally published in 1942, is set in the 1940s.

Durang, Christopher. *Beyond Therapy.* Nelson Doubleday, 1981.

A farce in play form presenting a man and woman who meet through an ad in a personals column.

Freedman, Benedict and Freedman, Nancy. *Mrs. Mike.* Putnam, 1947.

Sixteen-year-old Kate O'Fallon falls in love and marries Mountie Mike Flanagan, sharing his rugged life in the northern Canadian wilderness.

Gaeddert, Lou Ann Bigge. *A New England Love Story: Nathaniel Hawthorne and Sophia Peabody.* Dial, 1980.

A true-life old-fashioned romance is highlighted in this joint biography of Nathaniel Hawthorne and Sophia Peabody.

Garden, Nancy. *Annie on My Mind*. Farrar, 1982.

College freshman Liza Winthrop recalls the joys and sorrows of her high school senior year, when she and Annie Kenyon fell in love with each other.

Gingher, Marianne. *Bobby Rex's Greatest Hit*. Atheneum, 1986.

In a warm, funny novel about growing up in rural North Carolina in the 1950s, Pally has a crush on Bobby Rex, who represents all her dreams of adventure—even while she finds her strength in the bonds of home.

Hamilton, Virginia. *A Little Love*. Putnam/Philomel, 1984.

Sensitive Sheema feels fat, slow, and insecure, but she is loved both by her grandparents and by her strong, tender boyfriend Forrest, whose solid support enables her to make peace with herself.

Hannay, Allen. *Love and Other Natural Disasters*. Atlantic-Little, Brown, 1982.

Nineteen-year-old Bubber Drumm, who feeds road-killed armadillos to his pet tiger, falls in love with the 35-year-old mother of his ex-girlfriend.

Jordan, June. *His Own Where*. Crowell, 1971.

Written in lyrical black English, this is the poignant story of New York City teenagers Buddy and Angela, who love and nurture each other in a harsh world.

Kellogg, Marjorie. *Tell Me That You Love Me, Junie Moon*. Farrar, 1968.

A funny and poignant story of three physically disabled young people—Junie Moon, disfigured by acid; Arthur, a victim of a progressive neurological disease; and Warren, a paraplegic—who set up housekeeping together.

Kerr, M. E. *I Stay Near You*. Harper/Charlotte Zolotow, 1985.

Three linked stories tell of love over three generations in a small industrial town. Other Kerr novels about young people in love include: *If I Love You, Am I Trapped Forever?* and *Little Little*.

Klein, Norma. *Family Secrets*. Dial, 1985.

Family friends since childhood, Leslie and Peter become lovers in their high school senior year, but their relationship is strained when their parents divorce and Peter's father marries Leslie's mother.

Lee, Mildred. *The People Therein*. Houghton/Clarion, 1980.

In the southern Appalachian Mountains in the early twentieth century, the love between lame Lanthy Farr and a wandering naturalist from Boston, Drew Thorndike, overcomes the distances between them.

McCullers, Carson. *The Ballad of the Sad Cafe and Other Stories.* Bantam.

In a tragic triangle of obsessive love in a small, dreary southern town, the rich and harsh Miss Amelia is loved wildly by cruel Marvin Macy—but she loves the small hunchback Cousin Lymon, who does not love her. The story was originally published in 1943.

Mahy, Margaret. *The Catalogue of the Universe.* Atheneum/Margaret K. McElderry, 1986.

When beautiful Angela's dream of finding her father is shattered, she reaches out in her pain to her brilliant friend Tycho. This story makes the struggle for love and knowledge thrilling, funny, and mysterious.

Marzollo, Jean. *Halfway down Paddy Lane.* Dial, 1981.

Kate, a twentieth-century fifteen-year-old, wakes up in 1850 New England as the oldest daughter of an Irish immigrant family and falls in love with Patrick, who believes he is her brother.

Mazer, Norma Fox. *Someone to Love.* Delacorte, 1983.

During her first year at college, Nina moves in with college dropout Mitch in this novel that portrays the emotional seesaws of their relationship—their intimacy, fights, good times, and problems. Also by Mazer is *Up in Seth's Room.*

Michaels, Barbara. *Shattered Silk.* Atheneum, 1986.

In Michaels' latest romantic suspense novel, Karen Nevitt, a young woman on the brink of divorce, seeks refuge in the home of her aunt in Georgetown but instead finds sinister enemies among old acquaintances.

Myers, Walter Dean. *Motown and Didi: A Love Story.* Viking Kestrel, 1984.

Two Harlem teenagers, both determined in different ways to defeat the drug culture and poverty surrounding them, fall in love despite the barriers they have raised for protection against the pain in their past and present.

Peck, Richard. *Father Figure.* Viking, 1978.

When teenage Jim's mother dies and his estranged father returns, Jim competes with his father for the woman they both love and for the nurturing of Jim's little brother. Peck has also written *Secrets of the Shopping Mall* about two runaway teenagers who find a new life when they hide out in a suburban shopping mall and *Close Enough to Touch.*

Pei, Lowry. *Family Resemblances.* Random, 1986.

Teenage Karen learns from her unconventional aunt and from her own intimate experience about the sad secrets of adult passion and uncertainty.

Sachs, Marilyn. *Thunderbird*. Dutton, 1985.

A funny and touching "high/low" love story, in which Tina, a car-crazy high school senior, and Dennis, a conservationist library page, anger—and interest—each other.

Sallis, Susan. *Only Love*. Harper, 1980.

Terminally ill paraplegic Frances, feisty and passionate, meets bitter accident victim Lucas in a home for the disabled, and the two fall in love.

Shange, Ntozake. *Betsey Brown*. St. Martin's, 1985.

Betsey Brown, full of dreams to change the world, struggles with her loving but conflict-torn family in this lyrical portrait of three generations of black women.

Singer, Marilyn. *The Course of True Love Never Did Run Smooth*. Harper, 1983.

When longtime friends Becky Weiss and Nehemiah Barish get leading roles in the high school production of *A Midsummer Night's Dream*, they soon find themselves caught up in a romantic web as tangled as that in the play.

Smith, Betty. *Joy in the Morning*. Harper, 1963.

This is the story of young married love in a midwest college town during the 1930s in which an eighteen-year-old bride and her twenty-year-old husband struggle with problems of finance, education, and pregnancy.

Ure, Jean. *See You Thursday*. Delacorte, 1983.

Sixteen-year-old Marianne Fenton expects the worst when she learns that the new lodger, 24-year-old Abe Shonefield, is blind, but he turns out to be a pleasant surprise.

Willey, Margaret. *Finding David Dolores*. Harper, 1986.

Arly remembers herself at thirteen, fighting with her nosy, loving mother and obsessively following a handsome older boy.

Yolen, Jane. *The Gift of Sarah Barker*. Viking, 1981.

When they fall in love, Sarah and Abel are caught between the enlightenment and security offered by their Shaker community and an awareness of their awakening sexuality and need for affection and independence.

Young Love in Films

Breaking Away (1979): Limestoned out of their minds, four horny boys go for broke in Indiana.

Fast Times at Ridgemont High (1982): West Coast youth growing up too fast.

The Getting of Wisdom (1980): Australian film about a Victorian girls' school.

Gregory's Girl (1982): Scottish film about a young boy infatuated with a female soccer star.

A Little Romance (1979): Marvelous movie of youthful romance.

My Brilliant Career (1975): Australian film about a sixteen-year-old girl who wants to become a writer.

Peppermint Soda (1979): French valentine to the bittersweet joys of adolescence.

Saturday Night Fever (1978): Disco.

4 ♦ Planning Your Program

s you have seen from the Courtly Love program, a good program reflects the personalities of its designers. As it is implemented, the program should also leave a lot of room for involvement by the people who will be its intended audience. Just as the humanities reflect what it means to be human, likewise, good humanities programs naturally reflect the personalities of the program designers—you, the colleagues you will be working with, the scholars, and the young participants who will invest time and energy as the audience of your program. The intimate interrelatedness of people and ideas is what brings humanities programming to life.

As you yourself travel further into the creative process of program design and implementation, you should not overlook the need to balance your own initiative as project coordinator or leader with the necessity of working with others. After all, programs—by their very nature—are group activities. There is no reason to think that you should do everything alone. And, likewise, someone needs to be the point person, the coordinator. As you will discover, you will need to listen to other ideas when your own get muddled or run out; and others will need you to keep the entire project moving forward, however small or large the ambition behind the design.

A Clear Focus

The key to any successful young adult program (including humanities programs) is to focus on a topic that will interest and appeal to the young adults in your community. Of course, it might be easier to select a topic that appeals to you; but what about the young people in your service area? Will they be interested enough to attend the subsequent program?

Take a minute to consider the young adults in your community. Who are they? What activities are they involved in? The sample one-page survey (figure 1) reflects some of the questions you might ask as you develop a quick profile of your library's service area and the young adults in it. This profile can be a basic tool as you begin planning programs, and it will also help you plan for overall young adult services. You might already have some of this information in your library. Organizing it now will help you develop your program more easily.

Surveying the needs and interests of YAs in their communities is something young adult librarians do all the time, perhaps without realizing it. You read newspapers and other materials like school newspa-

School _____ Grade _____ Age _____ Sex _____

Why do you come to the Library? (Check as many as apply) For library programs _____ To get a book to read for fun _____ For material for school assignments _____ To hang out with my friends _____

When do you visit the library? (Check as many as apply) After school _____ Weekends _____ Summer _____

How often do you visit the Library? Never _____ Rarely _____ Monthly Every week _____ A few times a week _____ Only when I have a school assignment that requires it _____

How many books did you read just for fun this month?_____

Why do you choose the books you read for fun? (Check as many as apply)
__ Recommended by a friend   __ TV/movie   __ Browsing at public library
__ Recommended by a parent   __ Saw ad   __ Browsing at school library
__ Assigned by a teacher   __ Liked cover __ On a reading list
__ Recommended by a librarian

List your favorite author(s) _____
List your favorite book(s) _____
What is your favorite type of book? (Circle one):   Love stories   Humor
Mystery   Science Fiction   Horror   Fantasy   Adventure   Real-life Novels
Animals   Sports   History   Other (explain) _____

What magazines do you read regularly? _____
Do you subscribe to these magazines?   Yes   No
Do you read them at the library?   Yes   No
What book would you recommend to a friend? _____

What record, tape, or disc would you buy today? _____
What is your favorite radio station? _____

Do you belong to any clubs at school? (Please list) _____
Do you belong to any clubs outside of school? (Please list) _____
_____

How do you find out about things to do or see in this community? _____
_____

How do you get to community events and the library? _____

What kinds of programs would you attend at the library? (Circle as many as apply):   Films   Photography or writing contests   Book reviews or discussions
Sports   Crafts   Music   Other _____

Please write any comments you may have that would help the library plan services and programs for teenagers: _____
_____
_____
_____

Figure 1. A Survey of the Young Adults in Your Community

pers, yearbooks, and special interest publications. These tell you what young people are reading, doing, and talking about. Much of this informal surveying happens when you talk to young adults, either as a result of answering their questions or as part of conversation.

Many YA librarians have successfully tapped into the natural networks of their young patrons by forming focus groups involving a number of YA patrons. Such focus groups can be an extremely efficient and enjoyable way to find out what interests and concerns a representative group of teenagers. You can also tap into other community youth and school organizations. Would they be interested in working with the library? The best way to answer this question is to talk to teachers, school librarians, and youth service workers. Visit the school and community organizations, and ask whether they will help you by having their young people complete your survey. By involving schools and other youth service organizations, you are building a resource network and a constituency for the library and your programs.

You also need to know what resources your community can supply to programs. These resources might include collections of books, pictures, local memorabilia, audiovisual materials, historic documents and artifacts, meeting rooms, and special equipment (see figure 2).

Your first and most important resource is, of course, your library itself. Does it have enough appropriate materials to support a program? Have you considered a cooperative program with local schools so you can share resources? Can you borrow materials from neighboring libraries or the state library? Is there a local business or community organization that can supply additional materials?

Library staff people are another essential resource. Members of the library staff may have talents you can use. Of course, if yours is a one-person library, you will have to look for support from the community itself. Look at the organizations, educational institutions, and associations that are active in your area. Could they help sponsor or support a program? You will need people who can help you plan, promote, and produce your program.

Speakers and program presenters will not be selected until your planning has progressed, but you want to be aware of people who might serve in these capacities. A local college or university might provide you with the scholar that will make your program a success. Other resource people could be drawn from local organizations, city or state government, social service agencies, museums, and so forth. We have provided a checklist to help you organize your information-gathering process in locating resources. If your town seems to have very few resources, don't be discouraged. Cast your net more broadly and see who is available in neighboring communities and throughout the

I. Organizations and associations (Please list as many as you can)
Youth:
Business and professional:
Civic:
Political:
Cultural:
Religious:
Educational:
Ethnic:
Other:

II. Check those groups listed above that you think would be the most helpful to your library project.

III. List institutions found in your community. (Include a note on any special resources or materials available at that institution.)
Museums:
Historical societies:
Colleges and universities:
Schools (special classes, facilities):
Commercial enterprises:
   Performing arts groups:
   Auditoriums:
   Other:
Historical monuments:
Craft guilds:
Art galleries:
Churches and synagogues:
Publications (newspapers, magazines, etc.):
Media (radio and television stations):
Zoos:
Other:

IV. List scholars in your area who might be interested in participating in your program.

V. List resource people who may help you plan, promote, and produce your program.

VI. List individuals, businesses, or organizations that might make a financial contribution to a library program.

Figure 2. Locating Resources in Your Community: A Checklist

state. If you are planning a humanities program, funds are available from the state-based humanities councils and from NEH to pay for resource people for your project. But first start locally. You may be surprised to find a wealth of exciting and interesting resource people in your own community.

Surveying the young adults in your town and locating resources may seem like a great deal of work, but it is well worth the effort. Information you gather now will form the basis for all your planning efforts. It can also prove to be a valuable tool for planning and organizing other library activities, and it can be updated regularly. No matter how you use this information, the work will not be wasted. By the time you finish your community survey and resource assessment, you will probably have a good idea about the kind of program you want to develop. Pull together all the information you have gathered, and continue the program-planning process.

The Planning Group

The greatest temptation at this point is probably to sit down and completely design your own program. Why bother with a planning group? You can do it better and faster by yourself, right?

Wrong! After the preliminary work of roughing out a theme and the humanities issues you might deal with, planning in depth is a group process. You'll find that other people and groups will have valuable suggestions to make and that their contributions will result in a much richer program. Further, when you involve other people in the planning, you can be more certain that the resulting program will appeal to and interest your audience.

Who Should Be in the Planning Group?

Obviously, you and perhaps some other library staff members will play a major role in the planning process. In addition, representatives of the library board, Friends of the Library, and any institution, agency, or organization that is going to work with the library in sponsoring or producing the program should be actively involved in program planning.

Other members of the planning group may include the following: *Someone who is familiar with the topic on which you want to focus.* This could be a scholar, but it also may be someone in the community who has a special knowledge in the subject area, such as an attorney, a physician, a musician, and so on. *A scholar from an appropriate field.* The scholar can help the planning group focus on the humanities issues and clarify the value questions the program will cover. *Representatives of your target audience.* You have probably identified a particular segment of the teenage population that will be particularly interested in or affected by your program. Invite one or more young people from that target audience to become members of the planning group. Also use young adults who belong to clubs or organizations that reflect your program's topic, such as a school history club, a debating society, or a jazz club. If you have a young adult advisory board or review group at your library, ask members for suggestions or invite representatives from these groups to become involved. Young adult participation in program planning is essential. *Representatives of local cultural or historical associations, the local media, and other community groups.*

You may end up with a large group, but based on the results of your local resource analysis, you should be able to identify the best people to get involved. Keep in mind that you want to find people who will actively work with you during the planning stages and who will encourage young people to attend the program.

What Should the Planning Group Do?

The planning group should be a decision-making body. Although you have probably already developed some ideas about your program and consulted with a scholar about these ideas, the group will react to your presentation and help refine the ideas and make final decisions. It will help set the purpose and theme of the program, define the target audience, outline the objectives, identify the resources, and design the implementation of the program.

When you first contact the people you have selected for your planning group, you will briefly explain your ideas, the role and responsibilities of the planning group, and the date for the first group meeting. You may make the initial contact by phone, but it is a good idea to follow up with a personal meeting and a letter confirming the group member's willingness to participate, along with an outline summarizing your discussion. Your next step is to organize the planning meeting.

The First Planning Meeting

Begin by preparing an agenda of the topics you want to discuss at the meeting. If you have done your homework, this should not pose any problems. The agenda should cover the following areas:

1. A brief analysis of the local community and how that analysis relates to your program ideas.

2. A rationale for your library's involvement in the program. Explain how the program will benefit the intended audience and how it will enhance the role of the library as an educational institution.

3. A presentation of any ideas or suggestions you have for program topics, formats, goals, and so forth.

4. A review of the purpose of the National Endowment for the Humanities, its goals, and the types of programs it funds. This step not only helps prepare for the process of requesting funding, it also reiterates the essential goals of the humanities and library programming. If you are considering asking for funding from your state-based humanities council, it may have brochures that describe its purpose, goals, and funding criteria and that could be distributed at the meeting.

5. A group discussion of all these points. It is important to have both a recorder at the meeting to take notes and a facilitator (not you) to move the group process along. This is the time to note group members' ideas, criticisms, suggestions, and comments. At this point, also, it is important to find out whether the group participants or the agencies they represent can and will support the program. For example, in the area of publicity, imagine that a printer is part of your group. Can the printing be done for free? At cost? If the printer is from a busy city agency, will there be any problem using that service or any problem in going outside the public agency for private jobbing? Or perhaps a representative of the Junior League is part of your group. How will the League get involved if it supports the program? What presentations and support materials will you need to provide this member in order for her to present your program as something her organization will want to support?

If the group is interested and eager to support your program, you may want to proceed immediately with the next step. However, it may be better to organize a second meeting to handle the specifics of planning so that group members have some time to digest the ideas on the table and come up with additional suggestions. It would be especially helpful to group members if they could have the notes from the first meeting in advance of a second meeting.

As a follow-up to the five points above, or as the agenda for a second meeting, the planning group needs to answer these questions:

> What will be the *purpose* of the program?
> Who will be the *target audience?*
> What will the program do? What are its *objectives?*
> How will the material be *presented?*
> How will the program be *evaluated?*

Therefore, subsequent meetings will focus on who will administer the project, the selection of specific formats for the program, the selection of speakers, promotion and publicity, and the many details that must be worked out to run a successful program. You will need to find out, at the beginning of the planning process, the amount of time that group members are willing to give to the process and whether they and the institutions they represent have any financial resources in cash or in cost sharing to contribute to the project's budget.

A Word on Getting Approval

One of the early steps in planning is to get the approval and support of all agencies that will be involved in the program. You will need to present your ideas to the library's board of trustees or other governing bodies, as well as appropriate library officials, for approval and permission to pursue your project. You should also talk with any community group, agency, or institution whose help you will need to plan and produce your program. If representatives of these groups are on your planning committee, be sure that they will secure their organizations' official sanction for the program. You need to know how much support you can count on. If you ignore or overlook getting the approval of these groups, not only can it affect the success of your program, but it can also damage the effectiveness of the library's services. *Don't try to go it alone.*

Building an Audience

One of the most subtle yet significant aspects of the entire planning process involves understanding that audiences create themselves naturally around common interests of their individual members. Audiences do not exist as prepackaged entities. They form, often mysteriously and surprisingly, because someone has presented an opportunity that has intrigued individuals into coming to see what it's all about.

It is at this stage of planning that program designers encounter that intangible human element *energy*. People respond to boredom by yawning or turning away. People want to be involved, to feel enthused and energized. Nobody comes to a lecture to fall asleep.

Where does this energy come from in the case of humanities programs? It emanates from the excitement and enthusiasm of the program designers. If you are bored by the program design, the chances are very good that you will bore others with the program. So much of good programming is a marriage of practicalities with intangibles. It is not so daring, perhaps, to present a program on tax preparation—that is a program that will have an audience almost as soon as the posters and the thumb tacks meet the bulletin board. But a program on Courtly Love in the Shopping Mall is going to have a level of ambition that, in turn, will require lots of practical groundedness *and* lots of daring and boldness.

Really, what we mean here is that you should be having fun creating this thing called a program. Good programming is a source of excitement to an audience because each audience member senses that whoever put together this program was interested, involved, excited, and on fire with the idea. People want to feel passionate about something in life—in a subtle way, you model that desire by having undertaken the design and implementation of your program. If you and your planning group are not excited by the ideas underlying your project, how will an audience be stimulated to participate? Young people are given to lots of natural enthusiasm and excitement—so how will you bring these people together in your library to participate in a humanities program?

If you have never had programs for young adults at your library, it will take some time and effort to make teenagers aware that the library can be a place where they can come for special events such as programs. Be patient—you will undoubtedly find that your audience will grow with each new program you present. Therefore, it is probably best to present a series of programs rather than a one-time-only event. Keep your programs as simple as possible, and gear them to popular rather than academic tastes. Film showings are often a good way to begin programming for young people. A well-known film will usually draw a good audience; and, if you have the proper equipment, it is a fairly easy program to produce. For example, if you are fascinated by myth and heroes, it makes sense to bring your audience along; you may want to sponsor a program in which teenagers discuss the *Odys-*

sey, but you might begin with a film like *Star Wars*, which is replete with heroic figures, battles between good and evil, love interests, stereotypes, monsters, and so on, before you plunge headfirst into Homer.

Publicity is always important. You need to get information about your program to as many people as possible. (Specific details about planning and implementing promotional campaigns for library programming follow later in this chapter.) One of the best ways to build an audience is to involve young people in planning and producing your program. When people have an active role in planning a program, they are more likely to attend the program and bring their friends. Involve the youth clubs and organizations in your town. Draw them into program efforts as early as possible. Even those people who will not be able to take an active role will be pleased that they were asked to participate, and they may be interested enough to attend your program. By reaching out to many people, you stimulate interest and word-of-mouth promotion for your project.

In any case, from now on, you will want to keep returning in your planning sessions to the idea of *who* the audience is for the program and *how* the audience will be enticed into coming.

Turning Your Theme into a Program

Your planning is now under way. You have met with the planning group and have consulted scholars. You have outlined the issues that concern young people in your community. You have targeted the audience you want to reach. Planning committee, librarians, and scholars—together you have selected a theme for your program. Now you need to determine how you will achieve the goals you have set for your program. In chapter 3, we included some demonstration programs for your information. You can use these as models for your own program ideas.

Selecting a Suitable Format

There are many program formats from which to select when designing a program. We have prepared a list of suggested formats that you may wish to consider. This listing illustrates the advantages, equipment needs, costs, and possible limitations of several popular formats for humanities programs (see figure 3).

The planning group will help you select the appropriate format for your program. This process, like the matter of building an audience, needs to reflect both the practical and the inspirational. Your group, therefore, needs to be grounded in common sense when it comes to costs, projected audience, library schedules, and so forth, while at the same time it must allow the format to maximize people's desire to be excited by learning. Combine formats or add ideas of your own to come up with the format or formats that best fit the needs of your program's themes and goals.

The National Endowment for the Humanities encourages discussions among scholars, other program presenters, and the audience. The format you select for your humanities program should also serve to stimulate discussion. You want to involve the audience and challenge it to explore the issues and themes presented.

You should also work closely with your scholar and the young adults in your planning group to clarify the topics and issues that are involved in your program and to choose the best method for presenting its topic. Some of the points that need to be considered in selecting the best format for your program include the following.

How Do You Want the Topic to Be Presented?

What kind of reaction will the format bring? Will it allow for adequate exploration of the issues? Will there be real communication between the audience and the program participants? Will the format make the subject of the program come alive for the audience?

What Resources Are Needed for the Program?

The equipment, facilities, personnel, and other resources needed to produce a program are critical. Are there enough of these resources in the library or in the community to support the program?

Who Is the Target Audience?

Will the format you select attract and involve the young people you are trying to reach?

How Much Will the Program Cost?

Do you have the funds available to produce the program? If you are receiving funding from NEH or a state humanities council, do you

Figure 3. Selecting Program Formats

Format	Cost	Special Features	Advantages	Possible Limitations
Film*	Rental fee or borrow.	Requires projector and operator. Allow additional time to select and preview film.	Usually draws a good audience. Many excellent films to choose from. Easy to plan and present. Can present information and add emotional impact.	Must be previewed. Film can break or may not arrive; therefore, have a back-up presentation. Combine with another format to ensure that audience can participate in discussion.
Lecture*	Speaker's fee.	Need amplifiers if large room. Allow additional time to select speaker.	"Name" speaker can draw a good audience. Can present information tailored to program and audience.	Success depends on skill of speaker. Make special arrangements to ensure dialogue between speaker, humanists, and audience.
Dramatic Reading*	Minimal (unless professional actors are used).	Requires "readers". Allow time to select readings and rehearse performers.	Involves more people in program. Interrelationship of audience and actors can stimulate discussion.	Sometimes difficult to find appropriate readings. May be hard to find readers or coordinate their activities. Make arrangements to involve audience in discussion.

	Cost	Special Requirements	Advantages	Disadvantages
Videotape*	Cheap to rent, if available.	Special equipment.	Inexpensive way to present "name" speakers. Many humanities programs have been produced in this format, so they can be used again.	May be hard to find equipment. Small screen may be hard to see; several large monitors needed for a large audience. Make special arrangements to involve audience in discussion.
Panel, Debate, Symposium	Minimal unless some speakers are paid.	Allow extra time to select and brief speakers and moderators.	Presents different points of view. Can focus more clearly on issues, approaches, analysis. Can be a good discussion stimulator.	May be hard to find well-matched speakers. Speakers have a tendency to give long speeches rather than debate. Difficult to control; can get off course.
Projects, Field Trips	Varies.	Special planning.	Gives participants first-hand experience. Cooperative action leads to good interaction between participants.	Requires extra time for planning and arrangements. May be difficult to relate to humanities theme. May appeal only to a limited group. Hard to avoid "problem-solving" approach.

(Continued)

*These formats can be used successfully when combined with discussion periods during the program.

Format	Cost	Special Features	Advantages	Possible Limitations
Live Dance or Music	Minimal unless professionals are paid.	Props/costumes. Amplification. Talent.	Can attract large audience. Interaction of audience and performers can aid discussion.	Takes extra time and equipment. May be hard to relate to humanities theme. May appeal to limited group. Can be hard to "hold" audience for discussion.
Crafts, Other Demonstrations	Cost of materials.	Materials and other arrangements vary with event.	Can be linked with related library materials to attract nonusers. Can attract large audience if activity is popular. Good audience participation is possible.	Difficult to relate to humanities and public policy issues. May be difficult to locate teachers and equipment. Programs may duplicate those offered elsewhere.
Exhibits	Varies.	Installation. Exhibit space. Insurance.	May draw in nonusers. Requires minimal planning time and program personnel. Can be used to work with other institutions and groups.	No direct discussion. May not attract interest; no way to record attendance. Generally effective only when used with another program format.

Book Discussion Groups	Minimal.	Selection of books. Discussion leaders.	High level of group participation. Stimulates discussion of issues and critical thinking about books. Relates well to humanities and libraries.	Suitable only with small groups. Takes extra time to select books. May be difficult to stimulate interest in an activity that requires audience preparation.
"Buzz" Groups	None.	Need discussion leaders. Allow extra time to prepare.	Makes individual participation and discussion possible even in large groups. Excellent follow-up to speech or film. Possible to have several special interest focuses.	Discussion is not likely to be very deep unless leaders are well prepared. May require extra meeting rooms. May be hard to find willing discussion leaders.
Group Interview	None.	Need moderator or interrogator.	Brings out several points of view. Good audience participation through moderator. Adds air of informality to lecture or panel discussion.	Becomes disorganized without careful planning and a good moderator. Can be difficult to get audience reaction without strong introduction.

(Continued)

Format	Cost	Special Features	Advantages	Possible Limitations
Role Play	None.	Preparation of roles and directions to performers.	Good method of illustrating issues and problems if well handled. Generally good discussion stimulator. Can bring out factors and attitudes that might be ignored.	Can be stiff. Situation enacted can seem oversimplified or stereotyped. Tricky and difficult to use even if experienced.

have the required matching support from the library or other local sponsors? Will the program justify the expense?

Consider all format alternatives and their limitations before making your final decisions. You will want to keep all of the pros and cons of each format in mind as you continue planning so you will be prepared to cope with any problems that may arise. You should also note that some of the formats listed above are specifically designed to facilitate discussion. You may want to use one of these in conjunction with another format rather than settle on a simple question-and-answer session. Many formats require discussion leaders. If you choose one of these formats, it is important that you find the right person for the position. A person who can facilitate discussion, encourage participation, and involve the audience is key. Your planning group may be able to make some recommendations.

Selecting Speakers and Performers

If you have decided to have a lecture, a panel discussion, a dramatic reading, or a debate, your next step is to locate the best program presenters. Consult with your scholar and your planning group to determine exactly what you are looking for and to solicit their recommendations. Also, go through your community resource file. Although you are not limited to speakers from your local community (an NEH grant will fund travel expenses for outside speakers), you do not want to overlook the excellent people in your own backyard. For example, if you are planning a dramatic reading or a musical presentation, you should consider the talent available in local school or college drama and music departments.

You or a member of your planning group should, if possible, observe a speaker or performer in action before you extend any invitation for program participation. So-called "big name" speakers and presenters, while useful for instant name recognition and publicity, do not always live up to their reputations, nor are they easy to observe firsthand if they are from distant cities. It is sometimes surprising to discover that the scholar and teacher at the local or regional university or college is a wonderful speaker and group facilitator. You need to weigh the pros and cons of name recognition, reputation, and other nonacademic qualifications, along with scholarly or expert qualifications, when you begin to choose your program participants.

Once you and your committee have made your final selection and have listed alternatives in order of preference, you will want to extend a preliminary invitation. Your final arrangements, if this is a grant-funded program, cannot be made until you have received notification of grant approval. Still, it is important to get your tentative program date on the presenter's calendar as early as possible. It will also help you set up your budget because some presenters may require specific fees while others require reimbursement for travel expenses.

As soon as you have received notice that your project has been funded or as soon as all the planning is complete (for projects not based on grant funding), you should contact all program participants. Put all of your arrangements in writing—date, time, place, service to be rendered, fee, and so on. It may be easier to discuss the arrangements by phone or in person, but it is imperative that you follow up the conversation with a letter outlining all the points you covered.

Schedule a meeting of all program speakers and participants prior to the actual program, if possible. You will need to discuss the topic of the program, the format, and any equipment needs the speakers may have. If the presentations are to be written, it would be helpful to get them ahead of time to help you prepare your press release (see the section on publicity in this chapter) and to help prepare discussion leaders. Ask all participants for biographical information and a black-and-white photograph. Both will be useful for publicity for the program and for program introductions.

Selecting Audiovisual Materials

Selecting audiovisual materials is much like selecting a speaker. You will want to determine exactly what your presenter's needs are, as well as other uses for the equipment, such as slide and music shows, displays, or electronic exhibits. Then find out what is available. You should consult audiovisual catalogs at the state library, local public libraries, local school media centers, and college and university libraries. The state humanities council may also be an excellent place to start. It may have its own collection of audiovisual materials relating to the humanities or may be able to recommend titles and sources. Commercial film and video rental agencies are also important resources. Charges for the rental of audiovisual materials can be covered by an NEH grant.

Always preview the material well in advance of your program. Some catalog descriptions can be misleading, and you want to be absolutely sure that the material will fit the theme of your program. Perhaps a particular film or video is too controversial for your town, is not appropriate for teenagers, or will not stimulate discussion. The difference between excitement, stimulation, and controversy can be subtle—and problematic for a humanities program. Material that might be successful in one community or with a particular age group might be totally inappropriate for another. You and other members of the planning group should decide.

As soon as you receive notification of funding for your program, make scheduling arrangements for the audiovisual materials. AV materials are in heavy demand, so the sooner you make your request, the better. Be sure to have a list of alternate materials in case you have any problem securing your first choice.

Exhibits, Displays, Booklists

Of course, you will want to tie your library's resources to your program. The library has material that will stimulate people to explore the issues under discussion, and you will want to make your users aware of these materials. One of the ways to do this is through displays and booklists. Prepare a booklist of titles that will complement your program theme. Then arrange a display of some of these books in the library. A special exhibit of crafts, photographs, memorabilia, and historical materials that illustrate the theme of the program could also be used to promote the program and point out the resources available in the library.

Because exhibits are an excellent way of attracting attention to library programs, you may want to set up exhibits both in the library and in other community meeting places. In the case of young adult programs, placing exhibits in schools or the local shopping mall should be explored. Be sure that posters, fliers, or brochures that give the full details of your program and library resources accompany the display.

Publicity and Promotion

A far-reaching and creative publicity campaign can be a key factor in the overall success of your project. Although neither you nor any funding agency is interested only in a head count, you should make every effort to see that the people who would be interested in your program have at least heard about it. This is going to take time and effort, but by coordinating your promotion plans early in the planning process, you will be able to get the word out.

A good public relations campaign will also increase awareness of the library. One of the nicest side effects of library programming is that it generates a lot of interest in all of the library's resources and services. If you do not already have a strong public relations effort in place, this might be a good time to get started.

The first place to begin planning your publicity efforts is the survey of young adults in your community. This will help you identify the channels of communication (newspapers, radio and television stations, local clubs, and community organizations) that you can use to get your message out. It will also help you select the people you will ask to serve on your planning committee, perhaps on a special public relations subcommittee. Remember, when you want to reach teenagers, you must use their communications channels.

Any public relations committee should be made up of people who are not only familiar with the young people in your community and with public relations, but are also willing to put time and effort into the project. The size of the committee will depend entirely on the size of your town, the complexity of the program, and the number of tasks that need to be accomplished. It is critical that each committee member understands his responsibilities and the timeframe in which these tasks must be accomplished. The project director should work closely with the public relations committee to see that all the elements of the campaign mesh with other project plans.

What the Public Relations Committee Does

Designs a Publicity Campaign

What image of the program do you hope to project? What kind of people are you trying to reach? What are the issues of the program to which you want to draw attention? What are the program's goals?

Sets the Style of the Campaign

Will it be funny, serious, sophisticated, folksy? Think about who you are trying to reach and the image you want to create.

Decides Which Channels of Communication to Use

Talk to the newspapers (including school papers) and the radio and television stations to find out what public relations materials they require and their deadlines. Contact officers or advisers of local youth clubs and organizations to arrange for a presentation at their meetings or an announcement about the program to appear in their newsletters or bulletins.

Establishes a Publicity Calendar

Timing is everything. You won't want to release information too far in advance of the program or too late to stimulate interest. Every community varies in its attention span. When to send out news releases and public service announcements is best determined by local news and media professionals, who probably have their own deadlines. They will also be good resources for publicity advice and guidance. Look for balance in your calendar so that community interest can be built and sustained before and during the program.

Approves Design of a Logo

A logo is a symbol of a project that people recognize easily. It can be a simple design, a common symbol, or a complex illustration, depending on what you are trying to convey. The logo should be used in all information about the project so that over time it becomes easily recognizable. The actual artwork can be designed by a local graphic artist or the art department of a local school. A competition for art students to design the project logo can be great fun and stimulate interest in the program. If you decide to borrow a symbol from another organization or a commercial enterprise for your logo, be sure to get the proper permission.

Sample News Release and Public Service Announcement

A news release (often called a press release) is a formalized statement on your agency's letterhead that tells local media, including the newspapers, the *who, what, where,* and *when* of your program. It typically contains the name and phone number of a contact person who can give interested media members further information or verification of the news contained in the release. In terms of content, the first paragraph should summarize the essential details of the program. Subsequent paragraphs should be concise but contain interesting details about the program in general, the subject of the program, the speakers, and the history of the project at the library. Often, news editors cut from the bottom toward the top, leaving only the barest of information in what ends up in the newspaper. See figure 4 for an example.

A public service announcement (PSA) is the information you give to local radio and television stations to read on the air. They are usually of a short, specific length: 15 seconds, 30 seconds, or 60 seconds—the local station manager will give you the exact length for which you are eligible, along with her station's guidelines. There is an art to writing these on-air pieces. The tone can vary from straightforward (the same tone as your press release) to highly dramatic. It does not hurt to work together with someone else in creating these PSAs. You might

---

February 15, 1990
From: Jane Williamson
        Public Information Officer,
        Carnegie Public Library
        555-2000

Contact: Emily Quinn, Project Director
           555-2100, ext. 24

For Immediate Release

Local Teens Will Fall for New Library Program
"Courtly Love in the Shopping Mall"

"Courtly Love in the Shopping Mall," a series of programs for teenagers, will begin on Friday, March 18, 1990 at 7:30 P.M. at the Carnegie Public Library, 20 Main Street. The J. D. Salinger High School Dramatic Society will present a series of short theatrical sketches that look at love, courtship, and teenagers from Shakespeare's time to the present day. Michael Jagger, a professor of American studies at Liverpool University, will introduce the program and lead the discussion.

Dr. Jagger is a respected authority on Shakespeare and his influence on rock and roll music and lyrics. Dr. Jagger's book *Satisfaction* was nominated for the 1989 Transatlantic Book Critics Aware in nonfiction. He is a frequent guest commentator on MTV.

The Carnegie Public Library has received a grant of $125,000 from the National Endowment for the Humanities to present exhibits, field trips, and reading and discussion groups for area teenagers over the next 18 months. "We are excited and honored to receive this major funding from NEH," said Library Director Gertrude Stine, "and we look forward to presenting exciting and interesting programs for young people at the library and throughout the community."

-30-

Figure 4. Sample News Release

Michael Jagger, author of *Satisfaction* and professor of literature at Liverpool University, will be the guest speaker at the Carnegie Public Library's program for teenagers "Courtly Love in the Shopping Mall" on Friday, March 18, 1990 at 7:30 P.M. The J. D. Salinger High School Dramatic Society will present a series of theatrical sketches from literature dealing with courtship, love, and teenagers.

Figure 5. Sample Public Service Announcement

even put together a creative task force of YAs to write a PSA. See figure 5 for an example.

Some Points to Remember

Your publicity should begin early—perhaps with the announcement of the first planning meeting or the award of a grant.

All publicity items must mention the funding agencies that support the program. NEH and state-based humanities councils will give you specific guidelines in your award letter.

Be careful when you use the words humanities, humanist, and scholar. Unfortunately, these words can be misunderstood or imply an academic approach that may not draw the interest of the general public. Rather than focusing on the humanities as such, talk about the issues that will be discussed. It is always better to say "Dr. Sam Jones, a noted author and historian" or "Dr. Sam Jones of the University of Oklahoma" than to say "Dr. Sam Jones, scholar."

Word of mouth can be your best publicity. Be sure that all committee members and planners are kept up to date on the progress of your project so that they can pass on the correct information to their friends and associates. Keep the entire library staff informed about all the steps in the program planning process so that they can answer questions and keep library users informed.

Be sure that all information on press releases, posters, and brochures is accurate. Check names, dates, places, spelling, figures. Then check again.

There is a story in almost everything you do. If you ask a local art club or school group to design your logo, arrange a display, or co-sponsor the program, try to get the local newspaper to do a feature article on this community cooperation. Your scholar may have the most comprehensive collection of political campaign buttons west of the Mississippi. This would make an exciting segment for the local news. Do not overlook any potential news or feature story.

Take advantage of PSAs for radio and television. Be sure to use the stations that teenagers listen to or view. Check with the stations early enough to allow for their own scheduling arrangements. A personal visit to the station will be more effective than a written request; it may even result in an interview that will allow you to describe your program on the air. If you have never written public service announcements or press releases, consult an expert in the community for help and advice. The local advertising club may be an excellent source for this kind of information.

Your news release should follow established journalistic practices. A press release should include the name, address, and phone number of someone whom an editor can contact for additional information. It should be written so that the most important items come first, with pertinent details and information arranged in descending order of importance. This way, the editor can cut the least important facts at the end of the release if there is not enough space to run the whole article. Releases should also use everyday language instead of technical language that the average reader would find incomprehensible.

Use your imagination. Different approaches work in different communities. Think about what your community has to offer, and use it! Think about the types of activities and publicity that appeal to the people in your town.

A good PR effort does not need to cost a lot of money. Publicity is an important part of your program. NEH and many state-based humanities councils realize this and will fund public relations costs as part of your project grant. You should allow for printing costs for fliers, brochures, special stationery, and other such items in your budget. The cost of designing logos, printed materials, and public relations efforts can also be borne by NEH. If you do not request funds for publicity from NEH, your own efforts locally can be used as part of your local matching funds.

Some Thoughts on Evaluation

As the planning committee develops the plans for your proposal, it should also plan methods for the program's evaluation. Many people think of evaluation only in terms of numbers. While it is true that you should keep records of attendance figures, the number of people involved in planning and implementing the program, and the number of scholars involved in all phases of the project, such numbers do not indicate the effectiveness of the program. The following questions will help you examine the quality of your program.

> Did you meet the *objectives* you set for the project?
> Did you reach your *target audience?*
> How effectively was the *scholar* involved in planning and implementing the program?
> Were the *young adults* who attended the program stimulated by it?
> Did the program *promote discussion* between the audience and the presenters?
> Did the program *stimulate community interest?*
> Was the *publicity* effective?
> Were the *physical arrangements* adequate?
> What would you do *differently* if you presented the program again?
> Do you think the library should *continue* similar program efforts?
> What *impact* will the program have on the community?

While evaluation forms are often helpful, particularly in assessing audience reaction (see figure 6), they are not the only tool you will use to evaluate your program. Personal reactions from the project director, the program participants, the planning committee, and perhaps an outside evaluator will be valuable. You also might try using a small discussion session or personal interviews to evaluate the project. You may want to plan a follow-up meeting of the program planners and scholars to discuss the effectiveness of the program. Be sure to have copies and summaries of audience evaluation forms for meeting participants. If you choose to use evaluation forms for program planners and participants, include some open-ended questions that will allow for each evaluator to express personal opinions. It also may be helpful to put together a small group of young adult program attendees and get them to talk about the program, its effect on them, and their recommendations for further programming at the library.

The NEH staff has guidelines for the kinds of evaluations NEH require from its grant-funded programs. It may even be able to provide some sample forms for you to use. Be sure that you talk with the staff about evaluation criteria before you make a formal grant application. When doing evaluation, it is important to keep in mind that you are evaluating the original objectives of your program. Evaluation will be invaluable to the library as it makes decisions about future programming, planning, and services. You should make every effort to determine what impact your program has had on the library and its role in the community.

In order to present the best programs possible, we would appreciate your honest evaluation of the program you just attended.

1. In your opinion, what was the best thing about this program?

2. What did you find least useful about the program?

3. Please evaluate the discussion group leader [or insert other appropriate presenter title].

4. Have you gained something by participating in this library program? If so, what?

5. What ought to be changed to improve the program in the future?

6. How did you hear about this program, and why did you decide to attend?

7. Any other comments?

8. Your age:

   How often do you use the Carnegie Public Library?

Figure 6. A Sample Evaluation Form for YAs

5 ♦ Writing the Proposal

ow that you have gone through a thorough planning process—thought through why you want to have a program, what you want to do in the program, how you want to accomplish it, and who you want to participate in it—you are ready to write a proposal for funding support.

For programs in the humanities, there are two basic sources of funding available to libraries: the state-based humanities councils and the National Endowment for the Humanities (NEH). As part of the program planning effort, before you begin proposal writing, you should investigate both sources and decide which you will apply to for funding support. State humanities councils support a variety of projects ranging in cost from $500 to over $30,000. They usually have mini-grants available for $1,000 to $1,500 that help fund reading-discussion and film-discussion programs. Many of the state-based committees also have media centers and a wide variety of films and videotapes dealing with subjects in the humanities that make excellent program materials. Contact the staff at your state humanities council, read the council's guidelines, and make sure that it funds programs in libraries for young adults. Most state-based committees provide a specific application form for project proposals, and their staff will be helpful as you write your proposal.

The National Endowment for the Humanities publishes guidelines for each of its departments and offices. Study the NEH "Grant Program Guidelines and Application Instructions" before you start planning your program or writing your application. Determine the support category for which you are applying, and make sure you fit the eligibility requirements. Go through the NEH guidelines and make note of the elements required in a proposal. Be sure you understand what is required of your library before you begin to write the proposal.

Writing a proposal takes a lot of time and resources. Generally, the larger the dollar amount of your request and the more ambitious your proposed project, the more hours it will take to write a good proposal. Don't wait until the last moment to begin. Be sure to note the date proposals are due to be received in Washington, D.C., and work backwards to develop a timeline so the proposal can be composed, typed, duplicated, and mailed well before the due date.

As you write, check the guidelines to make sure you are including all the necessary parts of the narrative. Plan on the process taking *at least* three weeks from the first draft to the final product. Keep in contact with NEH from the very first glimmer of an idea for a humanities program through the drafting of the proposal. NEH staff members are eager to work with you, reacting to your ideas, offering advice and support, and helping you keep the program within NEH's parameters for public programming in the humanities. Staff members can also advise you on putting a budget together and provide you with the names of other librarians who have presented successful humanities programs. By contacting other libraries with a track record in producing programs and by requesting copies of winning proposals, you can get a good idea of proposal organization and content, budget format, and staffing.

Once you have determined the funding source you are going to pursue and have reviewed that source's application procedure and proposal guidelines, you can begin the actual writing. It may be helpful, at this point, to review some of the basic points of proposal writing.

Review of Proposal Writing Basics

1. Define your project, and come up with a *title* that suggests or defines the subject of the program. It may also indicate how the program will be presented. You will want to select a catchy, provocative phrase (one word is usually insufficient, and a sentence is much too long for the public to easily remember). The phrase also must state specifically what the program will be about. For example, the title "Diversity with Dignity: A Conference on Bicultural Education" is intriguing, and it also explains the content and format of the program. (See the section on publicity in the preceding chapter.)

2. Develop the sections of the proposal that will make up the *narrative.* The narrative section of the proposal will generally include:

A statement of the purpose or the objectives of your program. What do you hope to accomplish?

A brief description of the intended audience. Who are you trying to reach, and why did you decide to reach this targeted group?

A detailed explanation of how the program will be carried out—that is, the process for implementing your project. What will the format(s) be? Who will participate in the program? What provisions have been made for involving the audience and the program presenters in dialogue? Be specific. Your plan of action should answer the questions of *who, where, when, why,* and *how* the program elements are organized. Include themes, names of resource people and presenters, and a timetable.

A statement of how the humanities will be involved in the program. What will be the role of the scholar(s) in carrying out the program? How can the humanities contribute to an understanding of the themes and issues your program will address? You may wish to ask the scholar(s) in your planning group to write this statement for you. The humanities content must be clearly defined as a major goal for your project.

Information on the need for this project and how the project was developed. Describe the program planning process. Why do you think the program will meet a need or an interest in your community? Include a list of planning committee members and their specific roles in the creation and development of the program. Their vita should be included in the appendixes section of the grant application.

A brief description of your library and any other institutions or organizations supporting the program. You will want to stress why the library is capable of and interested in presenting the program. Include information about the library's service area, budget, staff size, and history of producing educational programs and of community involvement.

A description of your plan for promoting the project. This should include methods for attracting an audience and a description of all printed materials and public relations plans for the program. This is a key area; don't scrimp on detailing it.

A method for evaluating the program. Who will do the evaluation? What methods will be used? How will the final evaluation be used in determining future programs and services at your library?

3. By this time, you have a fairly accurate idea of what is going to be involved in your project. Now you have to figure out exactly what all this is going to cost and prepare the *budget.* Budget realistically and accurately. As you write the proposal, put the budget together so that you can keep track of what items you will need and what staff is necessary to produce your program. Include in-kind match and cost-sharing figures that represent your library's commitment to the project. Get accurate estimates of what it costs to hire a secretary, print a poster, and rent equipment and space, as well as fees for speakers, travel, per diems, and so on. Make sure your library cost-sharing figures really reflect all the time, staff, space, and other items or services that will help make your project work. Do not underestimate the amount of financial support you request or your library's cost-sharing contribution. Producing a project always takes more time than you anticipate.

At this point, you must also make a final decision about who will administer the project. Will you act as project director, or will you need to ask for funds to hire someone else to fill this role? Will you need clerical support, and will this support come from the staff, or will you need to hire someone? The planning committee will probably continue to oversee the project, but an individual must be in charge and able to work on the project on a regular basis.

If you apply for a grant from the National Endowment for the Humanities, your library will be expected to provide a 15 to 20 percent cost share of the total cost of the project. The state-based humanities councils usually require the local sponsor to put up matching funds or in-kind contributions on a 50-50 basis. In both instances, this cost share may be provided in the form of actual cash support; but, generally, matching funds are provided through in-kind support, which can include:

> *Staff services.* Will the library be paying all or part of the salary of the project director or other staff members working on the project? Will others in the community volunteer their services to support the project? For example, if you supervise the project director, the percentage of time you spend overseeing her work is in-kind support to the project.
>
> *Office space.* Is the library or another community organization donating office space for the project staff? If so, figure out the number of square feet times the average cost of office space in your community for your cost share.
>
> *Planning committee.* After the proposal has been funded, will the members of the planning committee continue to donate their time for meetings or other project activities?
>
> *Telephone.* Will you be using the library's telephone for local and long-distance calls related to the project?
>
> *Supplies.* Will the library or a local business or community agency provide all the office supplies for the project?
>
> *Printing.* If the library does not have a print shop, can a local business assume all or part of the printing costs as a public service?
>
> *Equipment rental.* Will the library provide typewriters, film projectors, or other audiovisual equipment that you would otherwise rent?
>
> *Meeting rooms.* Will the library or another community agency provide rooms for planning meetings or for actual programs?
>
> *Publicity.* Will a local photographer supply time or materials to publicize the project? Is a local writer or artist providing services to promote the project? Will the library's public information officer be working to promote the project as part of his regular duties?

As you can see, matching funds and in-kind services are not hard to find. Be specific about what you are able to supply, and most importantly, keep accurate records of the time, services, materials, and money that your library and other people and community agencies have donated to the project.

Budgeting is an important part of the program planning process and of proposal writing. The budget you develop for your project should reflect your project's goals and plan for implementation. Don't shortchange any item. With rising costs brought on by inflation, it may be hard enough to estimate your costs accurately without trying to cut down your estimates. If you do have to pare down your budget to fit the grant donor's financial guidelines, be sure to make corresponding changes in your planned activities. Too many projects run into trouble because the planner tried to do too much on a small budget. If you have questions when developing the budget—whether about how much to pay a speaker or scholar or about in-kind match or hiring staff—check with NEH or the state-based humanities council's staff. Either can be helpful about typical or prevailing rates.

4. The *appendixes* are an important part of the proposal. This section should contain support documents that add credibility to the proposal narrative. Include resumes of the project staff, planning committee, and participating scholars. Resumes should be concise (two to three pages) and current. Letters of support from cooperating organizations and institutions are essential and should be included in the appendixes. These letters should state an organization's role in the proposed project and its willingness to cooperate with the library if the project is funded. The scholars who have agreed to take part in the project as lecturers, advisers, discussion group leaders, and so forth should be asked to submit a letter stating their commitment to the project. It is helpful for the proposal writer to draft a sample letter of support and commitment and to forward this to the organizations and scholars so that they can see what needs to be included in their letters. Be sure to give the organizations and scholars enough time to get their letters back to you to meet the proposal deadline. Although it is not necessary to overload the appendixes with letters of support from members of Congress or other notable individuals, relevant materials—like the ones described above—will add substantially to the impact of the proposal.

5. Be sure to fill out the necessary *forms* contained in the application packet. These may include a cover page, budget forms, nondiscrimination certification, and others. Put the application together in the

order called for, and send in the required number of copies in time to meet the deadline.

Putting on the Program

You've got a grant! (Or your well-endowed library is ready to support your every budgetary need!) Now you're ready to set the gears in motion and get your program going.

First, set up the financial and accounting parameters of the project with your library's budget officer. Make sure the project budget is clearly understood and a system is developed to keep track of in-kind contributions and cost-sharing obligations.

If your project calls for the hiring of staff, do so. Be certain to put the contractual agreement between the library and the project staff in writing. Detail salary, duration of contract, duties, and hours. It is critical that both the project staff and the library understand what is expected of project personnel.

Bring your advisory committee together, review the goals and objectives of the project, and start to firm up program plans. This may be a good time to set the calendar for your programs (you probably put together a tentative calendar during the planning process). Confirm the dates and times after checking to see if these will yield the best turnout. Make sure your participating scholars and speakers are still available. Check carefully for potential conflicts with other local or national events. Even an excellent program will not draw an audience if everyone in town is attending the annual county fair or watching the Super Bowl.

Contact all of your program personnel, and put all your final arrangements in writing. If you need to make travel arrangements, make hotel reservations, or schedule or rent equipment and meeting rooms, be sure to solidify all the details as soon as possible. Again, make sure to put all the arrangements in writing. Misunderstandings and mistakes are more likely to happen if the details are not down in black and white.

Get help if you need it. You may want to appoint a person or a committee to handle specific tasks as you prepare for the program, but the project director must oversee all activities and make sure that all jobs are done. If you are not acting as the project director, be sure that the person you hire fully understands all the responsibilities involved in the job and all the authority delegated to her. (In the appendixes you will find sample job descriptions for various project personnel.)

There are some administrative activities that can be delegated to committees or individuals. These are:

> Publicity and promotion
> Displays and support materials
> Speaker and equipment arrangements
> Facilities (reserving and setting up meeting rooms)
> Finances
> Supplies
> Registration procedures
> Evaluation

We have put together a planning checklist that will help program directors outline the various tasks that must be accomplished before and after each program (see figure 7). If assigning these tasks to a committee, the director should be sure that each committee member understands exactly what his or her role is and the deadline by which the task must be completed.

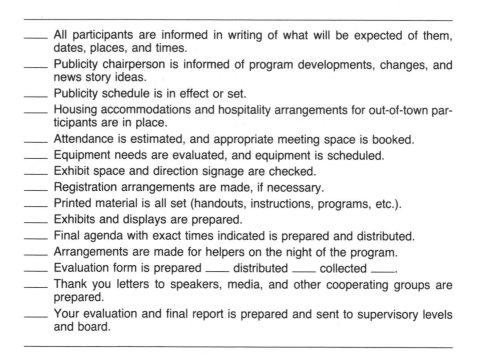

____ All participants are informed in writing of what will be expected of them, dates, places, and times.

____ Publicity chairperson is informed of program developments, changes, and news story ideas.

____ Publicity schedule is in effect or set.

____ Housing accommodations and hospitality arrangements for out-of-town participants are in place.

____ Attendance is estimated, and appropriate meeting space is booked.

____ Equipment needs are evaluated, and equipment is scheduled.

____ Exhibit space and direction signage are checked.

____ Registration arrangements are made, if necessary.

____ Printed material is all set (handouts, instructions, programs, etc.).

____ Exhibits and displays are prepared.

____ Final agenda with exact times indicated is prepared and distributed.

____ Arrangements are made for helpers on the night of the program.

____ Evaluation form is prepared ____ distributed ____ collected ____.

____ Thank you letters to speakers, media, and other cooperating groups are prepared.

____ Your evaluation and final report is prepared and sent to supervisory levels and board.

Figure 7. Planning Checklist for Project Directors (adapted from the Wyoming Council for the Humanities)

Where do you find people to serve on these committees and help out with your programs? Begin with your original planning group. Many of the members will have already volunteered their services and experience. They can also probably suggest others who might be interested in getting involved. You could ask other library staff members, Friends, and volunteers for help. Look through your community resource file for people or groups that might be interested in helping with these activities. Only you and the project director will know how many extra hands are needed. Pick people who are reliable, able to meet deadlines, and interested in working with the library.

There are several advantages to involving many people in producing and publicizing your program. First of all, it reduces your workload. Though you (or the project director) will still have final responsibility for the program, there will be others to help take care of the details and create excitement and interest in the program. And people who are actively involved in a program are more likely to attend the event and bring their families and friends.

6 ♦ Measuring Success

ong, long ago, says an Eskimo story, there was no difference between people and animals. Animals could become people if they wanted to, and people could be animals. There was one common language in those magical days, and words had amazing power. A word spoken by chance might have strange consequences. It would suddenly come alive and what people wanted to happen could happen—all you had to do was say it. Nobody could explain this: That's the way it was.

The role of the inexplicable in the humanities—of the *great mysteries of life*—is well represented by the significance of question asking, as we see frequently in our sample programs. We come full circle now to the humanities themselves, especially, as essayist Gregory Stevens pointed out earlier, to the interrelatedness of humanities to language itself.

If our culture has given rise to language that reflects itself, the words *success* and *failure* are active yeasts indeed. How do we evaluate whether our humanities programming efforts with YAs are *successful?* As the Eskimo story seems to warn us, "Carefully!" Because the word *failure* has such a strong aftertaste, it can overwhelm any careful recipe. While we certainly can arm ourselves against our fear of failure by plans, steps, and all the processes of working together that provide us a measure against failing, still, ultimately, we just never do know for sure how a program will turn out.

That is the gamble. Maybe it won't work. But, as the Eskimo story teases us, what we want to have happen *can* happen. *Success* is one of those loaded words that have crept like Bermuda grass into the garden of the American mind. If perception creates reality, maybe all we need to do is say a program was a success and—hocus pocus—it *was* a success! If that's how it worked in the old Eskimo days . . . Well, therein lies a humanities program on ethics and ethnics.

We can do something to make provisions for success—we can work, and we can take steps and prepare. Yet there is an element of magic to all this, though we would be fools to believe that there exists some sort of magic wand. This book is not a magic wand. It is a guidebook with a big disclaimer: Beware of those selling roadmaps to the humanities! Beware of the dread humanobabble, the jargon with tongues for hair! You'll meet strange Sirens on the road to programming, and not one of them will sing the same song about what constitutes success.

We suggest you think about each program you do for your library as one in an endless series—for, in truth, you don't know how many programs you will do. The road is an endless one, as Odysseus discovered, because the human journey is not yet complete. Let it stay that way in order that you can gauge the success or failure of one particular program in a realistic light. The word *failure* has a way of killing one's desire to take chances, and face it—good programs in the humanities require taking lots of chances. For starters, if you have never done a program, that in itself is a lot of risk taking to wager in hopes of succeeding.

How do you evaluate something like a program? How do you measure success in a world of ideas that are hard to measure? We advise you first to be wary of loaded terms like *success* and *failure*. Find more helpful terms, but do not flinch from a need for honesty. After your program, or at some point during it, you can ask, "What did this program accomplish? What did not work so well?" Tom Phelps, director of Humanities Projects in Libraries and Archives, National Endowment for the Humanities, passes along this suggestion: "The true measure for public education through libraries is whether or not participants came to know something more about a subject, came to a better understanding of a theme or topic, or came to appreciate human works or ideas."

Certain practical evaluations can naturally be formulated, based on a number of criteria: attendance, use of library collections, evaluation questionnaires returned by participants, and evaluation by scholars of how they saw things. You can measure and quantify how many books your program used, how many people sat in chairs, the circulation of publicity materials, newspaper press coverage, and so forth. You will get feedback from participants through evaluation forms and word of mouth, phone calls, and letters. Solicit comments—how else will you really get a sense of what you achieved through the program? Attend some sessions. You can tell a great deal about your presenters and your participants by watching. Where there's heat, there's fire; where there's excitement, enthusiasm (and people express enthusiasm in all kinds of ways), and enjoyment, there has been a transaction in the learning process between people. Ask the scholars, the board members, and librarians on duty during the program for feedback, written and oral.

What you cannot measure is the effect that programs have on a community, for ultimately, the real success of a program is whether it satisfies the need of individual participants to delight in learning, along with the need for people to be part of a community of ideas.

Finally, whatever else you may conclude in your evaluation, did you enjoy yourself? What did you get out of it? And remind yourself frequently, especially when you get frustrated, that nobody else took the risk of making up from scratch the program you guided along into reality. Remember that you wanted something to happen for your young patrons and for your library. You tried it.

We wish you the rewards of that experimentation. For humanities programming is open ended; nothing is final, and no question results in the ultimate answer. Our desire to help, to learn, and to enjoy good company and good ideas is the real boon to the unsung heroes of libraries. May all that you try lead you to the next great program idea.

7 ♦ A Possibility for Further Humanities Programming

regory Stevens and Michael Bell are two scholars whose interests in their respective disciplines (Stevens is a classicist, Bell a folklorist) took them into interesting partnerships with public libraries. Both have helped formulate humanities programs for YAs. In this chapter and the next, we present two additional demonstrations to give you ideas for designing your own YA programs.

B.P.O.P. (Big Person on the Planet) and the Heroic Catalog

by Gregory I. Stevens

Big Person on the Planet. One pictures Tom Hanks in the movie *Big* fulfilling a wish many of us experienced as young adults: to grow up quickly, to be a big person. The charm of *Big* comes from our ability to identify with one of the major dilemmas of adolescence—growing up (who would not like to spend a lifetime developing toys and games and just playing?). Movies such as *E.T.*, *Big*, *The Chronicles of Narnia*, *Alice in Wonderland*, and many others focus on that one central dynamic: childhood and its future legacy. Why do these video adventures hold such a powerful sway over us? What do these creative expressions tell us about our diverse cultures and ourselves? Where does this material come from?

As we start to answer such questions, we are embarking on a journey into the humanities. Questions involving our cultures inevitably are interpretive: how do we make sense of our world? In seeking answers, we are traversing the humanities; our discussions with young adults range over topics such as (1) the search for meaning (identity); (2) the living past (heritage); (3) art and the aesthetic experience; (4) the social web (institutions); and (5) language (in all media, including video). These five descriptions have been offered by Ernest Boyer, president of the Carnegie Foundation for the Advancement of Teaching and former U.S. Commissioner of Education, as the key to an integrated general education program. They represent collectively how the humanities expand our worlds by giving us new ways of seeing ourselves and our place in the world.

This essay was prepared by Gregory I. Stevens, assistant dean, College of Humanities and Fine Arts, SUNY, Albany.

In young adult programming, we seek to provide as many access points as possible for the audience we want to reach. Many of us, through training or habituation, are very book centered. Yet we may lose out on an opportunity to connect with young people if we do not involve "texts" that are beyond the book. The venerable Socratic technique begins with nothing more than starting at that point—not where you are, but where the audience is. That may explain why movies centering on children are so popular: everyone has the experience in common. The humanities, in providing access points to the audience, seek to enlarge upon the shared experience by increasing our stock of experiences and by appealing to our sensibilities to see the particular in general.

The movie *Big* is informative on this point. We could say that we shall look at all wish-fulfillment literature in which children project themselves as adults. Sounds pretty academic, doesn't it? But if we use a theme such as "Power and Position," we have escaped the academic verbiage and provided a hook that is accessible and that allows us the freedom to plan, with young adult assistance, a program that opens the circle. If we wish to narrow the focus slightly, we can call the program "B.P.O.P. and the Heroic Catalog."

Given the number of times young adults watch things (MTV, movies, videos, etc.), we would be well advised to find a humanist who is up on film (such resource people might exist in art, English, sociology, anthropology, communications, or film studies). If we are going to work with multimedia, someone from literature, comparative literature, or humanities will be a plus. Here again, if the topic is sufficiently open, we allow various humanities scholars the opportunity to become involved.

On the other hand, if all we do is watch films and read books or use other "texts," we will not have a humanities program. We need some framework in which discussion and dialogue can occur. The humanists, working with your advisory committee, should identify themes that can be orchestrated in terms of the overall program topic and that can be "personalized" by the group. Personalization of the theme means that the theme is relevant to the audience, that each person can see an individual access point by which to become an active participant in the process. Participants can also be asked to perform an outside activity to share with the group (a catalog of related country and western music, comic books, sit-coms, rap music, etc., in addition to the more familiar books and films). You may wish to involve a foreign-language specialist to talk about how a person gains insight into foreign cultures by using the authentic materials approach.

Let us suppose that at this point in our program development we have talked to a lot of humanists and young adults, and we have decided to implement "B.P.O.P." The program will explore concepts of the heroic, past and present. After a good discussion, the planning group decided to use the historical approach, ancient to modern. There was strong lobbying for a present-to-past version ("back to the future"), an approach that will be taken in the next program. Now that we were using the historical framework, we could both arrange the material using chronology and involve scholars where appropriate. Several common themes would be touched upon by the scholars, although their presentations would be in nonspecialist language:

1. The hero as culture bearer.
2. The hero as wish fulfillment.
3. The hero as child.
4. The hero as extraterrestrial.
5. The hero as survivor.
6. The hero as role model.
7. The anti-hero.
8. The hero as larger than life.

These eight themes were developed by our group. While some could be part of others, we decided to leave well enough alone and to avoid nitpicking.

The group now saw that several humanists would need to be involved: a historian, an anthropologist, a couple of people from literature and film, a philosopher, and a sociologist. The group agreed that, if necessary, the philosopher, anthropologist, and historian could carry the program by themselves. Potential scholars were then asked to write a brief essay discussing the topic vis-à-vis their areas of expertise and especially identifying "texts" (including film and music) and projects that could be used with young adults. The young adults on our committee were asked to read and respond in terms of the three A's: access, attraction, and appropriateness.

The committee then felt comfortable with the components of the program and began thinking of ways to create interest in it. One thing it decided to do was to publish, in slick wrappers, an essay on the program to be given out in the library and to local teachers, school board members, library trustees, and journalists. The essay that follows, "Where Have All the Heroes Gone?," is an overview and hints at questions the program will explore.

Where Have All the Heroes Gone?

What is special in a culture? How does that uniqueness become recognized and institutionalized, if not enshrined? How receptive, and in what ways, does an audience need to be before a hero or heroine can emerge? Are heroes more likely to emerge in an age of social, political, or religious repression? Is heroism a natural, characteristic expression of human potential or of what we think human potential ought to be? The program on "Where Have All the Heroes Gone?" will explore the dimensions of these questions with humanities scholars and young adults.

No matter how we define the term, the *heroic* is inextricably tied to our notions of human potential. Whether we project ourselves into animal forms to give them our attributes or to assume theirs (Richard the Lionhearted or the coyote, known among American Indians as The Trickster) or we make extraterrestrial forms human-like (E.T.), our baseline is the human being. Simply put, we want to understand what we wish for.

A culture gets the heroes it deserves and needs. We find ancient relics like the pyramids of ancient Egypt and ancient rituals concerning hero worship, and because of the things that a society preserves, we can see that the society's aspirations, expressed through its heroes, are of paramount importance. Within this historical approach, ours is not an easy task because the availability of evidence for an interpretation decreases as we travel back in time. We should not expect to find an equal number of male and female heroes. Obviously, in societies dominated by one sex, the other is subservient. That is why more ancient literature was written by men than by women. The power relationship between the sexes determines who has access to education and to the great texts or their creation.

As a function of maintaining the separation between the sexes, physical abilities and capabilities linked to male and female become noticed and preserved through the ages in the divinities created to support each sex. From this simple projective technique, Western civilization subsequently accepted gender roles based on physical attributes and power. In societies where weapons represent power, like the Roman Empire, men have weapons. In societies where words and writing are power, as in ecclesiastical Rome and Lutheran Germany, men have the scribes and printing presses. Whatever basis of power was first used for gender differentiation, by the dawn of recorded history—that is, history recorded by men—there is no notion of equality. The ancient Athenians went so far as to call women *oikouremata*, or stay-at-homes. The equality of women as seen in their ability to leave the house in Aristophanes' *Lysistrata* was probably the biggest joke of the play at the time.

It is no surprise, then, to see that the denigration of women goes hand in hand with the hero worship of men through the Western world. If women in antiquity are heroic, it is because they assumed the sex-linked attributes of men. In other words, Wonder Woman is really androgynous because she displays Herculean male attributes from within the female shape.

To study any age's heroic catalog, then, we must be mindful that the values of our age are not the same values as those of times gone by. The lens of the late twentieth century through which we look at heroes and heroines of antiquity may be colored by variables that influence and bias our sightlines and interpretations. On the other hand, ancient civilizations afford us the most opportunity to view the discrete aspects of heroes and heroines. So whether we start with *Gilgamesh* or the Old Testament, we can grasp the monolithic work as though it were one piece. As we proceed to the present, we are less and less likely to see the materials all at one time.

The earliest heroes, as we would expect, fight adversaries easily recognized and understood by all people: mortality and marauders. In terms of thematic developments, the heroic catalog can be read backwards: find a major threat to a culture, and you will then find the appropriate hero to combat that particular threat. Another way of looking at this is to say that each hero is specialized in terms of his/her/its idiosyncratic power, physical or intellectual. Hercules' twelve labors are those physical tasks that an agrarian society found tremendously onerous, while Oedipus gets to be king by solving just one riddle. In addition, a role model may embrace one quality so pervasively that the person's name itself stands for the trait: Penelope, Judas, Midas, Snow White, Einstein.

In his book *The Hero in History,* Sidney Hook makes an interesting distinction in his determination of who deserves heroic status. He talks of the "eventful man" and the "event-making man." According to this scheme, the hero who gains his status accidentally (for example, the Dutch boy who put his finger in the dike) is not really worthy of the title. Rather, the event-making person, the one who changes history directly by calculated intervention, is the one who deserves the accolade.

If we pursue Hook's distinction, we find that the heroic concept gets harder to trace as we proceed to the end of the twentieth century. How many event-making people are we willing to call heroes? What will be their specialties, or what are the common perceived threats that our culture wishes to vanquish? How will we know what the threats are, given the diffuse nature of our culture and the proliferation of media-conjured events? Who can tough it out convincingly, given our own heterogeneity?

It must have been much easier for earlier ages, with their homogeneity, to create requisite heroes for any occasion. If there could be one common strand or general concern running through the creation of the heroic catalog, it would be the notion of perfection—if not perfection in everything, then perfection in one given arena (strength, intelligence, artistry, etc.). The ideal of perfection is pervasive in the West, as in the Garden of Eden, Eldorado, and other utopias. It might also follow that we are less patient with the less than perfect. Is our culture more concerned with the language of failure or with the language of success? Do we allow our heroes the opportunity to make a mistake? Is perfection the goal of human development in the same way that the vision of the Grail is the culmination of an Arthurian knight's existence and final virtue?

With the recognition that perfection is difficult for humans to attain comes the creation of rationales for its elusiveness, such as loss of grace, the fall, and the Tower of Babel. If humans, or even gods, cannot be perfect, what can they do or be to be selected out for the admiration of others? Can we create heroes who "just say no"? Can we frame a positive charge to the light heroic brigade?

Even a superficial historical analysis points out the problems associated with the term *heroic*. Early societies were not open societies. Did the slaves and serfs have their own heroes? Of course, the slaves and serfs had no power and hence no means of extolling their aspirations (except through Christianity and other transcendent religions where belief and faith create the ideal of a better life after this one). More latent in ancient and other cultures is the idea that all people are not equal and that some people, by lot or divine plan, occupy a permanent niche in the social structure. It is not difficult to see how the notion of an eternal reward evolved. Again, our perspective on the collective past is influenced by our own ideas on personhood and autonomy of choice.

Accordingly, it is not surprising that the ancient Greek heroes Achilles and Odysseus are more accessible heroes than is Aeneas. After all, Achilles had expressed his choice before he went to fight at Troy: given the alternatives of either a long, uneventful life or a short, glorious one, he chose the latter. And offered several possible lives during his return from Troy, Odysseus chose to return home. Aeneas, on the other hand, does not choose his future, but is commanded to follow a divine, preordained plan. Of course, the cultures in which these heroes appear explain why the characters must be the way they are. In ages where physical survival is fraught with peril, there is great fascination for those who have the resources and the prowess to reach old age.

To pursue further the ancient examples, we can see that in a society that is highly individualistic, the heroes are individuals themselves who stand alone, head and shoulders above the rest (like Odysseus and Achilles). On the other hand, in civilizations where the concept of statehood, empire, or kingdom is the chief concern, the heroes reflect more abstract values such as patriotism, nationalism, or social altruism. Some heroes are self-directed, and others are other-directed. One way to organize the heroic catalog would be to look at the beneficiaries of heroic action.

As we get into recorded history, we see a shift from the individual hero who is above the crowd to the collective hero who is one of us. When we talk of the founding of a country, we usually find one individual who is credited with being the father of the land—Aeneas for Rome; George Washington for the United States. And why not? If Aeneas and Mr. Washington had lost their causes, we should have had different values for our founding conceptions. The heroes and mythologies of settled states reinforce and solidify the values on which those states are built. Where can we actually read what Uncle Sam did? But we do know who he is.

With King Arthur in the Middle Ages, we find an unusual array of talents at the Round Table. The heroes of this time are sworn to a code of ethics, courtesy, and behavior beyond modern belief. The search for the Holy Grail (wonderfully sent up by Monty Python) required the utmost purity and devotion. Why? The times required an antidote to the picture of English life we get a little later in Chaucer's tales.

English life in the countryside must have been terribly uncouth, rugged, and foul. Sometimes heroes are endowed with characteristics exactly opposite those commonly found. The Arthurian legends may have evolved as a means of encouraging a reaction against all the negative habits and manners of the time or as a consequence of the country mouse-city mouse dialogue.

The key behavior of the hero-as-one-of-us is sublimation, channeling one's real need for immediate satisfaction into a search for an almost intangible, lofty, ethereal, ennobling spiritual goal (such as the Grail, used by Christ at the Last Supper, or the unattainable woman in the courtly love poetry of the medieval period). There seem to have been, throughout history, many attempts at controlling the impulsive behavior of young men. One of the more permanent solutions was to send them on Crusades where their aggressive natures could be directed toward chopping up infidels in the Holy Land. Even Zeus, the chief Greek god, is thought to have caused the Trojan War to relieve overpopulation and the intense competition among men for land and possessions.

From the Renaissance to recent times, heroes usually have been people like us who have given themselves to a cause or calling. Some were religious heroes or martyrs, people who believed to the point of death in the correctness of their visions (like Joan of Arc). Others, such as the early explorers and then the industrialists, believed in more worldly visions such as the amassing of wealth. With the interest in wealth came the interest in taking resources. This meant piracy and war. Heroism in these times was reflected in those who plundered with impunity (like Black Beard) and those who, representing acceptable national interests, won or lost major wars (like Washington and Napoleon). Combat became the proving ground for establishing a person's prowess and fame. Medals were created to award those who saved the homeland.

However, the twentieth century brought a more sobering view of war. With the advent of nerve gas (World War I), atomic bombs (World War II), and questionable causes for war (Vietnam), this arena has become much more constricted. Look at the differences in attitudes toward war in Crane's *Red Badge of Courage* (Civil War) and three twentieth-century poems: "The Trumpet," by Edward Thomas (1917); "Dulce et Decorum Est," by Wilfred Owen (1920); and "The Death of the Ball Turret Gunner," by Randall Jarrell (1945). Note how more recently aggression spawns sentiments of pacifism as well.

Today's concepts of heroism suggest a repetition of an earlier pattern, on the one hand, and a breaking away to alien concepts, on the other. An example of the former is the return to the Herculean figure who possesses physical prowess of astonishing proportions (for example, Rambo). As in past cultures, the emphasis is on ultimate good winning out over the forces of evil. The hero at the national level, even as the underdog (consider, for instance, the *Rocky* movies, Underdog cartoons, or Olliver North), must be ethical in order to be popular. This can be seen in the supernatural figure of E.T. or in any of the films where creatures disposed to do good (as in *Cocoon*) visit earth. Here, there is a strong messianic tone because the do-gooder is seen as a savior with not only superhuman strength, but profound wisdom.

In retrospect, it is clear that the conception of the hero is tied to the developments and values important to the hero's culture: that the hero is endowed with those attributes a given people wish to imitate or revere; that the hero may have traits different in kind (human or extraterrestrial) and degree (one of us, but with much more than we could ever have); that the hero embraces norms that show us the difference between right and wrong; that the hero, in many cases, does not suffer from pangs of mortality and is often construed as immortal (with the video medium, each superhero is literally ageless and immortal— James Bond is still alive and well); and that a hero satisfies the demands of a particular people at a particular time in a particular place.

Whether we assemble our heroic catalog from cartoons, books, real-life events, or other sources, we are working on the hardest puzzle of all: how easily can we discover who we are? The writers who bring us, in their works, heroes and heroines give us individual insights and glimpses into the larger mosaic of identity. By obtaining a knowledge of what others before us have thought, we move further along in our own quest for self-knowledge and self-fulfillment. It is not possible to remain a Gulliver or an Alice or a Candide forever; naiveté gives way to knowledge as each generation, through its own rites of passage, comes of age. For a hero to live, we must believe or want to believe in that hero's truth. Otherwise, we need to contemplate an unheroic age. It is the intent of this young adult series to open doors and minds to new ways of seeing.

Overall Theme to Be Explored

Gregory Stevens' premise is that each hero is a reflection of the age in which he or she lived or was created. Stevens encourages us to explore the many facets of heroism. We look to heroes of the past in history and literature in our search for role models. To come up with a catalog of heroes amounts to a kind of search for what we today hold valuable.

The purpose of this unit is to illustrate the heroic catalog through programs and to help young adults in this search for the values that will shape their lives. Using the essay, you can now generate ideas for library YA programs. We have selected some possible program topics for this sample unit, using the following humanities disciplines: classics; history; literature; history of art; philosophy; women's studies; religious studies; and cultural anthropology. You can approach these disciplines using the following questions:

> Who is a hero? Today? In the past? In ancient times?
>
> What characteristics do people generally admire? Do these characteristics change or remain the same in different historical periods?
>
> Do heroes reflect the times in which they live? Do some historical periods encourage the development of heroes? Do wars spawn heroes?
>
> In what ways do heroes reflect their cultures?
>
> Are there different types of heroes? Anti-heroes? Super heroes? Those who overcome great odds? Those who change history?
>
> Do some historical periods encourage heroism more than others?
>
> Why are there relatively few female heroes? How does this affect our concept of heroism?
>
> Is heroism a "masculine" characteristic? Can women only become heroic by assuming male characteristics?
>
> Is the seeker (for example, the seeker of spiritual enlightenment or justice) a heroic figure?
>
> How do the heroes we admire and follow shape our lives?
>
> Who are the popular heroes of young people today?
>
> Is perfection heroic?
>
> Do we need heroes?

Programs by Topic

With these questions in mind, we can now start sketching some programs by topics such as "Heroes with a Cause," "Heroes Then and Now," "Heroes at War," "Heroic Women," "Anti-Heroes," and "Supernatural Heroes." Below we have suggested some possible programs using a particular topic as a focal point. We have offered ideas for program formats, along with a perspective of the topics from the humanities point of view. Following the suggested topics, the last section of the unit provides a resource list of books and films that might be used in programming.

TOPIC: Heroes with a Cause

This program examines people who changed history because of their devotion to a cause.

Program Title: "People Who Made a Difference."

Format: Reading and discussion series.

Humanities Focus: Scholars in appropriate disciplines discuss the subjects' lives and contributions, stressing the ways each person had an impact on history. The speakers also help the audience to address the subjects' heroic attributes.

Scholar's Questions and Comments: How do these people compare with classical heroes? What characteristics or qualities do all these people have in common? Are these qualities you admire? Can extraordinary people lead ordinary lives? Or are they compelled to be heroes?

Books and Film: Emma Goldman, *Living My Life;* Margaret Mead, *Blackberry Winter;* Linda Atkinson, *In Kindling Flame: The Story of Hannah Senesh, 1921–1944;* Lenore Bennett, *What Manner of Man: A Biography of Martin Luther King, Jr.; Martin the Emancipator* (film).

TOPIC: Heroes Then and Now I

A comparison of heroes of the past with contemporary heroes.

Program Title: "The Hero in Pictures."

Format: A display of prints, photos, and posters that illustrate heroes past and present, combined with a guided tour of the exhibit by an art historian.

Humanities Focus: The exhibit will provide a springboard for discussion of the qualities and values that are heroic. YAs should be encouraged to discuss those qualities they think are important and to comment on the people they think of as heroes.

Scholar's Questions and Comments: What makes a hero? What heroic qualities do the various people represented in the exhibit embody? How do the graphic pieces in the exhibit express this? Is heroism displayed in different ways (by different motifs)? At various times in history? What qualities do you feel are heroic today? Does this exhibit show a changing pattern of heroism? If so, what is it?

TOPIC: Heroes Then and Now II

A comparison of past and present heroes.

Program Title: "Today's Heroes."

Format: Lecture and slides picturing important past heroes and contrasting them with today's heroes.

Humanities Focus: The purpose of this program is to consider whether the qualities that create a heroic figure have changed and to see whether the heroes young people admire today have an impact on their social and emotional development.

Scholar's Questions and Comments: The scholar should help the audience identify similarities and differences between the two groups of heroes. The scholar should cover such questions as: Why are these people heroes? Would you like to be like them? Are today's heroes different than those of the past? How do today's heroes reflect contemporary society?

YA Involvement: Hold a contest and let the teens select the men and women they consider today's heroes. Use these people in the series.

TOPIC: Heroes in War

Title: "Gone to Glory."

Format: Reading and discussion series or readers' theater readings of poetry about war.

Humanities Focus: Discussion should focus on the realities of war from literary and historical perspectives, from a young person's viewpoint before and after seeing combat.

Scholar's Questions and Comments: What is courage? What is worth dying for? Is war glorious? Can it be a proving ground for bravery? Have our attitudes toward war in general changed in the 200 years of our history? What is "real" heroism? Should you fight in an unpopular war (e.g., Vietnam)? One you feel is wrong? Are humans aggressive by nature or environment?

Books, Plays, and Films: Megan Terry, *Viet Rock*; Tom Cole, *Medal of Honor Rag*; David Rabe, *Sticks and Bones*; Walt Whitman's poems; Wilfred Owen's poems; Randall Jarrell's poems; *Red Badge of Courage*; *All Quiet on the Western Front*; *Three Comrades*; *From Here to Eternity*; *The Cruel Sea*; *Johnny Got His Gun*.

TOPIC: Heroic Women

Program Title: "First Ladies: Women Who Were the First to . . . ."

Format: Reading and discussion of biographies.

Humanities Focus: This series will look at women who were the first leaders of countries, leaders of causes, or leaders in fields of endeavor that have generally been dominated by men. The series will consider whether heroism changes when women are the leaders.

Scholar's Questions and Comments: Are women who have strong "masculine" qualities more likely to be heroes? What are these qualities? Are women more likely to be seen as heroes during times of repression? In more liberal eras? How do these women demonstrate their power?

Books: Rosalyn Fraad Baxandall, *America's Working Women: A Documentary History — 1600 to the Present;* Eleanor Flexner, *Century of Struggle: The Woman's Rights Movement in the United States;* Emma Goldman, *Living My Life;* Vera Brittain, *Testament of Youth;* Lillian Hellman, *Six Plays;* Marianne Moore, *The Complete Poems;* Rachel M. Brownstein, *Becoming a Heroine: Reading about Women in Novels;* Agnes DeMille, *Dance to the Piper and Promenade Home;* Laurie Lisle, *Portrait of an Artist: A Biography of Georgia O'Keeffe;* William Godwin, *Vindication of the Rights of Women.*

A Sample Bibliography

The following bibliography contains suggestions of popular reading for young adults on the subject of heroism and heroes.

Alexander, Lloyd. *The Kestrel.* Dutton; Dell, 1982.

Enraged by the death of his friend, young Theo becomes a great battle leader, a fierce and bloodthirsty animal known as the Kestrel-hawk; then a crisis shocks him out of his mindless brutality.

Angelou, Maya. *I Know Why the Caged Bird Sings.* Random, 1970.

This is a remarkable, poetic, and frank autobiography of a black girl who tells about growing up in Arkansas, St. Louis, and San Francisco.

Atkinson, Linda. *In Kindling Flame: The Story of Hannah Senesh, 1921– 1944.* Lothrop, 1984.

This is a biography of the young Jewish Resistance fighter, captured after parachuting into Nazi territory, whose spirit and courage inspired fellow wartime sufferers.

Auel, Jean. *Clan of the Cave Bear.* Crown; Bantam, 1980.

An orphaned Cro-Magnon child adopted into a clan of Neanderthal hunter-gatherers grows into womanhood feeling like an outsider, but she learns that her survival is linked to that of humankind.

Baldwin, James. *Go Tell It on the Mountain.* Knopf; Dell, 1953.

John's fight with his father is about the black man's view of himself; it is also about John's fight against his parent's self-righteous and brutal authority.

Bell, Clare. *Ratha's Creature.* Margaret K. McElderry; Dell, 1983.

Millions of years ago in a society of intelligent wildcats, Ratha is driven from the pack when she discovers how to tame fire and challenges the pack's leader.

Bennett, Lerone. *What Manner of Man: A Biography of Martin Luther King, Jr.* Johnson, 1964.

A journalist portrays Martin Luther King, Jr., and his role as leader of the American civil rights movement.

Brontë, Charlotte. *Jane Eyre.* 1847. Many editions available.

Orphaned and abused as a child, Jane grows up fighting to believe in herself, small, plain, and poor as she is. She gets a job as governess in a rich, great house and falls in love with its brooding, passionate master.

Brooks, Bruce. *The Moves Make the Man.* Harper (and paper), 1984.

Jerome, the first black to integrate a white school, knows the moves he needs to survive—in basketball and with people—but his fragile white friend Bix refuses to learn how to fake.

Brown, Claude. *Manchild in the Promised Land.* Macmillan, 1965.

The author gives a realistic account of his life in Harlem.

Cole, Brock. *The Goats.* Farrar, 1987.

A boy and a girl, known as "the goats" at their summer camp, are the victims of a cruel practical joke, but they escape and find shelter and self-respect as they take care of each other.

Conrad, Pam. *Prairie Songs.* Harper (and paper), 1985.

In the solitude of the wide Nebraskan prairie, young Louisa looks up to the sophisticated doctor's wife, Emmeline, but Emmeline cannot adjust to the harsh pioneer life—especially to the loneliness.

Cooper, Susan. *The Dark Is Rising.* Margaret K. McElderry; Macmillian, 1973.

Will Stanton is the seventh son of a seventh son, one of a special circle who must undertake a quest in the fight against the dark powers that threaten once again to take over the world.

Cormier, Robert. *The Chocolate War.* Pantheon; Dell, 1974.

Jerry Renault stands up to a brutal school gang and to the authorities when he refuses to sell chocolates to aid school funds.

Crane, Stephen. *The Red Badge of Courage.* 1895.

One of the features of warfare not clearly described by recruiters is the awful fear—a fear so strong as to make an enlistee run away.

Craven, Margaret. *I Heard the Owl Call My Name.* Doubleday, 1973.

As he lives and works among the Indian people in several remote Canadian villages, a dying young Anglican missionary becomes sensitive to the strains and the richness of their lives. This novel is spiritual without being preachy.

Cross, Gillian. *Chartbreaker*. Holiday, 1987.

Teenage rock star Finch is vulnerable and ugly, but she sings like concentrated danger, her performance charged with rage and her love for the band leader.

Dickens, Charles. *Great Expectations*. 1861. Many editions available.

An escaped convict—"a fearful man all in coarse gray with a great iron on his leg"—grabs young Pip in the graveyard and continues to haunt him as Pip struggles to become a gentleman.

Du Maurier, Daphne. *Rebecca*. Doubleday; Avon, 1938.

Poor, plain, and alone, a young woman marries a rich widower, but in his great English country house, she feels she cannot live up to his dazzling first wife, Rebecca—and then a terrible secret is revealed.

Elder, Lauren and Shirley Streshinsky. *And I Alone Survived*. Dutton, 1978.

This is the true story of a courageous young woman, the sole survivor of a plane crash in the High Sierras, and her grueling ordeal in the mountains.

Fast, Howard. *April Morning*. Crown, 1961.

A fictional account of the events of April 19, 1775, in Lexington and Concord from the perspective of 15-year-old Adam Cooper.

Ferris, Jean. *Invincible Summer*. Farrar, 1987.

Robin learns to face her leukemia with the help of a fellow patient, wise and gentle Rick.

Fox, Paula. *The Moonlight Man*. Macmillan; Dell, 1986.

Catherine has always looked up to the father she has barely known since her parents divorced when she was three; but, at age 15, she spends the summer with him and discovers his weakness and desperation.

Frank, Anne. *Anne Frank: The Diary of a Young Girl*. Modern Library; Doubleday; Pocket, 1952.

This moving journal was kept by teenager Anne during the two years that she, her family, and other Jews were hiding from the Nazis in a secret annex in Holland. *Anne Frank Remembered*, by Miep Gies, tells how Gies helped hide the Frank family.

Gaines, Ernest J. *The Autobiography of Miss Jane Pittman*. Dial, 1971.

Through the character of his compelling, 110-year-old heroine, Gaines interprets and personalizes the black experience in America—from slavery to the present.

Graham, Robin and Derek L. T. Gill. *Dove*. Harper; Bantam, 1972.

Sixteen-year-old Graham takes a five-year voyage around the world in the 24-foot sloop Dove.

Green, Hannah. *I Never Promised You a Rose Garden*. Holt; NAL/Signet, 1964.

In an autobiographical novel, Hannah Green (the pseudonym for Joanne Greenberg) describes the struggle of a teenage schizophrenic girl to leave her private fantasy kingdom.

Greene, Bette. *Summer of My German Soldier*. Dial; Bantam, 1973.

To help a German prisoner of war escape, Jewish Patty defies her abusive father and the prejudiced people of her small Arkansas town.

Halberstam, David. *The Amateurs*. Morrow; Penguin, 1985.

In a nonfiction account of four young men's quest for the 1984 Olympic gold medal in rowing, one of them says that, despite the arduous training, he enjoys being able to reach beyond himself, "the chance to be a hero."

Hall, Lynn. *The Solitary*. Macmillan, 1986.

After graduation, plain Jane Cahill returns to the backwoods cabin where she once lived and tries to find out whether it is terror or courage that fuels her quest for self-reliance.

Hamilton, Virginia. *The House of Dies Drear*. Macmillan; Dell, 1968.

Thomas discovers that his Ohio house was once a station on the Underground Railroad, from which some brave escapees went back into slavery to show others the way to freedom.

Hemingway, Ernest. *A Farewell to Arms*. Scribner; Collier, 1929.

In the muddle and horror on the Italian front during World War I, an American ambulance driver falls in love with a nurse and discovers that war holds little glory.

_____ . *The Old Man and the Sea*. 1952.

The very old and the very young celebrate supreme courage in a sea story.

Hershey, John. *The Wall*. Knopf, 1950.

A novel written as if it was the diary of a Jew living in the Warsaw Ghetto.

Holman, Felice. *Slake's Limbo*. Scribner; Macmillan, 1974.

Scorned and tormented at school and on the streets, orphaned Slake feels he is a worthless lump until one day he takes refuge in the subway where he makes a home.

Howker, Janni. *Badger on the Barge, and Other Stories*. Greenwillow; Penguin, 1985.

Five long short stories tell of young people who are helped at a time of crisis through an encounter with an old stranger.

Jenkins, Lyll Becerra de. *The Honorable Prison*. Dutton, 1988.

When Marta's father stands up to a terrorist Latin American dictatorship, the family is placed under house arrest in a remote region.

Jones, Diana Wynne. *Howl's Moving Castle*. Greenwillow, 1986.

Sophie, the eldest of three daughters, knows that according to fairy-tale convention, she is expected to fail first and worst, so she does not even try; but when a witch's curse turns her into a feisty old woman, she finds the energy to hobble out into the unknown.

Kerr, M. E. *Gentlehands*. Harper; Bantam, 1978.

Buddy likes his refined and cultured grandfather, who helps Buddy impress his rich girlfriend, until a shocking secret is revealed that stretches back to the Holocaust.

Kingston, Maxine Hong. *The Woman Warrior*. Knopf; Random, 1989.

Kingston describes her conflict growing up Chinese-American, caught between the "ghosts" of Chinese tradition and the alien values of the United States.

Leitner, Isabella. *Fragments of Isabella: A Memoir of Auschwitz*. Crowell, 1978.

The strength of the human spirit and the passionate will to survive degradation and death are portrayed with searing intensity in Leitner's fragmented memories.

Lipsyte, Robert. *One Fat Summer*. Harper; Bantam, 1977.

Overweight Bobby Marks slims down one summer as he sticks to an exhausting job, stands up to his father and the local bullies, and finds his own definition of a hero.

London, Jack. *Great Short Works of Jack London*. Harper, 1965.

Many of London's short stories, such as "Love of Life" (1905), are about one person or animal alone in the savage wilderness, struggling for the basic needs of food and shelter.

McKinley, Robin. *The Blue Sword*. Greenwillow; Berkley/Ace, 1982.

Kidnapped by the king of the mysterious Free Hillfolk, Harry Crew learns that she possesses untrained magic powers and that she is destined to follow in the footsteps of a legendary female warrior.

Mahy, Margaret. *The Changeover: A Supernatural Romance*. Margaret K. McElderry; Scholastic, 1984.

With the help of an older boy who loves her, Laura changes over into a witch to fight the evil forces that are attacking her little brother.

Malcolm X. *The Autobiography of Malcolm X*. Grove, 1965.

An important document of black history, this is Malcolm X's revealing personal account of life in the ghetto, in prison, and as a black Muslim.

Mason, Bobbie Ann. *In Country*. Harper (also paper), 1985.

As Kentucky teenager Samantha tries to find out about her father who died in Vietnam before she was born, it makes her wonder about herself and whether she would go to war and shoot to kill.

Mathabane, Mark. *Kaffir Boy*. Macmillan; NAL/Plume, 1986.

This autobiography of a black boy's coming of age in apartheid South Africa depicts a fierce struggle for survival under conditions of overwhelming brutality.

Maugham, W. Somerset. *Of Human Bondage*. 1915.

Medical student Philip Carey, born with a clubfoot, struggles for independence and becomes obsessed with a shallow young woman.

Meltzer, Milton. *Never to Forget: The Jews of the Holocaust*. Harper, 1976.

Based on diaries, letters, songs, and history books, this work is a moving account of Jewish suffering in Nazi Germany before and during World War II.

———. *Rescue*. Harper, 1988.

This is the story of how Gentiles—from Oskar Schindlker to Swedish Raoul Wallenberg—saved Jews in the Holocaust. Also by Meltzer is *Ain't Gonna Study War No More*, about pacifists throughout U.S. history.

Monsarrat, Nicholas. *The Cruel Sea*. Knopf, 1951.

The heroism and weariness of World War II at sea are told through the experiences of the men aboard a British escort ship that battled the German U-boats in the stormy north Atlantic.

Myers, Walter Dean. *Fallen Angels*. Scholastic, 1988.

Seventeen-year-old enlistee Richie Perry grows up quickly when he is faced with the savagery and sorrow of the war in Vietnam.

Nye, Robert. *Beowulf, A New Telling*. Hill and Wang, 1968.

Also published by Faber in England as *Bee Hunter: Adventures of Beowulf* (1968). Reprinted as *Beowulf, the Bee Hunter* (1972), this version of Beowulf versus Grendel is written for YAs.

Oneal, Zibby. *In Summer Light*. Bantam, 1986.

Home from school with mono, Kate drifts, lonely and irritable, unable to use her artistic talent and crippled by her rage at the famous and domineering artist father she once adored.

Orwell, George. *1984*. HBJ, 1949. Many paper editions available.

Winston hates the system and Big Brother. He knows that his rebellion puts him in terrible danger and that the Thought Police will find him.

Paterson, Katherine. *Jacob Have I Loved*. Harper; Avon, 1980.

Plain Louise feels that her pretty twin sister deprives her of school-ing, friends, a mother, and even her name.

Paulsen, Gary. *Hatchet*. Macmillan, 1987.

Brian struggles to survive alone in the Canadian wilderness after a plane crash.

Peck, Richard. *Father Figure*. Viking; NAL/Signet, 1978.

Jim Atwater's self-chosen role as substitute father to his younger brother is threatened when, on the death of their mother, their father returns.

Peyton, K. M. *Prove Yourself a Hero*. Collins; Dell, 1978.

After being kidnapped and held for ransom, Jonathan Meredith has a feeling of guilt and cowardice until he gets a chance to confront his captor.

Portis, Charles. *True Grit*. Simon & Schuster; NAL/Signet, 1968.

A stubborn fourteen-year-old finagles an equally stubborn marshal into helping her track down her father's killer in the Old West.

Potok, Chaim. *The Chosen*. Simon & Schuster, 1967.

The search for personal identity within the framework of a strong religious tradition is explored in this story about Jewish fathers and sons.

Pullman, Philip. *The Ruby in the Smoke*. Random, 1987.

In Victorian London, orphaned Sally Lockhart, age sixteen, alone, and uncommonly pretty, finds herself in deadly danger connected to a mysterious great ruby and the corruption of the opium trade.

Remarque, Erich Maria. *All Quiet on the Western Front*. Little, Brown, 1929. Many paper editions available.

Fighting in the nightmare trenches of World War I, a group of high school classmates realize that false patriots have sent them to fight for a cause they know nothing about.

Renault, Mary. *The King Must Die*. Pantheon; Bantam, 1958.

Small, quick-witted young Theseus must undertake a perilous journey to Athens to find his father and his own heroic identity.

Rylant, Cynthia. *A Fine White Dust*. Bradbury; Dell, 1986.

An intense revival preacher comes to town, and Pete is born again. He realizes he loves the Preacher Man, who seems fierce and mysterious and who asks Pete to go away with him.

Santiago, Danny. *Famous All Over Town*. Simon & Schuster; NAL/Plume, 1983.

Teenage Mexican-American Chato, gifted and sensitive, is pressured by the machismo of his father and the neighborhood gang in a humorous, moving novel set in Los Angeles.

Santoli, Al. *Everything We Had: An Oral History of the Vietnam War as Told by 33 American Soldiers Who Fought It.* Random, 1981.

Thirty-three veterans of the Vietnam conflict recount its impact on their lives one decade later.

Schaefer, Jack. *Shane.* Houghton; Bantam, 1949.

Young Bob Starrett loves the mysterious lone cowboy Shane, who helps the homesteaders in their conflict with the cattlemen in Wyoming in 1889.

Schulke, Flip. *Martin Luther King, Jr.: A Documentary . . . Montgomery to Memphis.* Norton, 1976.

Striking pictures and text graphically recapitulate the entire civil rights movement through the story of Dr. King's struggle to fulfill his dream.

Sillitoe, Alan. *The Loneliness of the Long-Distance Runner.* Knopf; NAL/Signet, 1960.

In a long short story, a teenager held in an English reformatory turns out to be a champion runner, but as he trains, he plans a perfect way to defy the powerful people who have always excluded him.

Solzhenitsyn, Alexander. *One Day in the Life of Ivan Denisovich.* Dutton, 1963.

In midwinter, in a Stalinist Siberian labor camp, brutality and degradation loosen a man's tenacious hold on his humanity.

Swarthout, Glendon. *Bless the Beasts and Children.* Doubleday; Pocket, 1970.

The misfits in a tough, competitive summer camp out west find self-respect when they work together to free a herd of buffalo about to be brutally slaughtered.

Townsend, Sue. *The Adrian Mole Diaries.* Grove; Avon, 1986.

Adrian Mole would like to be an intellectual hero, but he has all these mundane worries: spots on his chin, a girlfriend whose interest is waning, and parents who barely notice when he tries to run away.

Twain, Mark. *The Adventures of Huckleberry Finn.* 1885. Many editions available.

With fugitive slave Jim, outcast Huck Finn rafts down the Mississippi, away from those who would "sivilize" him.

Voigt, Cynthia. *The Runner.* Atheneum Ballantine, 1985.

Bullet runs ten miles a day and is state champion, but only cross country, never track. Fierce and apart, he is determined that no one will box him in.

Wersba, Barbara. *The Dream Watcher*. Atheneum, 1968.

Albert feels like a complete misfit at home and at school until his friendship with an elderly self-designated actress gives him the courage to be himself.

White, Terence H. *The Once and Future King*. Putnam, 1958.

A tongue-in-cheek portrayal of chivalry enlivens this masterful modern version of the life of King Arthur. Through fantasy, humor, and White's compassionate vision, legendary heroes are humanized, and the tragic grandeur of the Arthurian epic is given meaning.

Wright, Richard. *Black Boy*. Harper (paper also), 1945.

Wright's autobiography describes growing up in the racist South, where, though he was forced to mask his pride in himself, "It had never occurred to me that I was in any way an inferior being."

Heroics in Films

Cat: A Woman Who Fought Back. Producer: Jane Warrenbrand. Films Incorporated, 1978.

Cathy Davis is a boxer who successfully struggled to receive a license to fight professionally in the state of New York. This documentary portrays the people who opposed Cathy's quest, as well as her determined insistence on receiving this professional recognition.

Crossbar. Producer: Crossbar Productions. Learning Corp. of America, 1978.

This emotionally gripping film, inspired by the life of a one-legged Canadian high jumper, portrays a young man's great determination to pursue his goals despite his handicap and shows how he eventually proves his ability to jump with the best.

David. Producer: Leo Rampen, Canadian Broadcasting Corp. Director: Tom Kelly. Filmakers Library, 1979.

This is a documentary about an extraordinarily personable and self-sufficient teenager made all the more remarkable by his having Down's syndrome. With the help of his loving and supportive family, David has mastered many difficult tasks, including grace under pressure.

Fantabiblical. Producer: Bruno Bozzetto Film. Distribution Sixteen, 1978.

Based on biblical themes, this innovative and bizarre science fiction fantasy is highly imaginative and marked by a line of almost irreverent humor throughout, which may make it a sensitive film for audiences with fundamental religious affiliations.

Jump. Producer: Walter Clayton. Stryker Productions, 1978.

In a candid and introspective manner, nineteen-year-old Ruthy shares her experience of learning to sky dive. Descriptive footage of her training for and execution of her first parachute jump is matched by Ruthy's musing consideration of the motivation and trepidation of such a feat.

Mom and Dad Can't Hear Me. Producer: Daniel Wilson. Time-Life Video, 1979.

Afraid of rejection if her friends learn that her parents are deaf, Charlotte fabricates a series of protective lies, only to learn the value of genuine love and self-respect. The positive portrait of the deaf parents as successful and caring people reinforces the poignancy of this struggle for acceptance and understanding.

Pretend You're Wearing a Barrel. Producer: National Film Board of Canada. Phoenix Films, 1978.

This vivid portrait of describes 35-year-old, single parent Lynn Ryan who, determined to leave life on welfare behind her, takes a course in welding and, after many disappointments, finds a job that not only enables her to support herself and her five children, but also allows her to express a calm, dignified triumph.

Strange Fruit. Learning Corp. of America, 1979.

Loosely based on Lillian Smith's novel and set in a small town in Georgia in 1948, this drama focuses on a black painter who faces the ugliness of racism. At first avoiding involvement in a black registration drive, Henry Brown is moved to action and eventually takes a courageous stand that inspires his community.

Truly Exceptional People: Carol Johnston. Producer: Jim Thompson for Dave Bell Assoc. Walt Disney Educational Media, 1979.

Carol Johnston, an aspiring Olympic gymnast, was born with only one arm. Her remarkable determination and resoluteness as she pursues her athletic goal are conveyed in this inspirational film.

8 ♦ A Second Possibility for Further Humanities Programming

olklorist Michael Bell's fascination with urban folktales is the starting place for our third demonstration humanities program. His essay and possible library programs are presented below.

I Know It's True Because It Happened to My Best Friend's Cousin: The Modern Legend in America

by Michael E. Bell

Not long ago, a local police chief related the story of an attempted child snatching at a nearby shopping mall. The audience of concerned parents gasped as the chief described how quickly it happened. One minute the child was standing next to her grandmother. Several minutes later, she was missing. The panicked grandmother convinced the mall manager to lock all the doors. Within twenty minutes, police and security guards found the child. But during the short time she was missing, her abductor had cut the girl's hair and changed her clothes.

Is this story true? If so, how is it possible that the same story, with minor changes, is told throughout the country? Could this event have taken place in so many different places to so many different people? Whether such stories are true or not, why are they told? What is their meaning? What role do they play in the lives of tellers and listeners? How does this kind of story relate to stories that were told generations ago or to stories told now in other parts of the world? What are the different kinds of stories? How do these stories relate to modern society? Do they reflect our current fears, concerns, hopes, values, beliefs? These are just some of the questions about stories and storytelling asked by scholars is various disciplines, from history and literature to anthropology and folklore. The questions focus on evidence and verification, the processes of storytelling, continuity and change in story texts, the meanings, uses, and functions of stories and storytelling, the historic and geographic distribution of story types, themes and motifs, and the various forms of narration.

One folklorist has said that folklore, including the telling of stories, comes early and stays late in our lives. Even we sophisticated

This essay was written by Michael E. Bell, director of the Rhode Island Folklife Project, Rhode Island Heritage Commission, Providence, Rhode Island.

Americans have not been "unfolklorized," as another folklorist phrased it. Every generation seems to have its doomsayers who assert that folklore is dying out. During the past 50 years or so, this argument may have seemed particularly valid in light of significant and rapid changes in our culture and society and, perhaps most evidently, in our technology. Yet it may be that these cutting-edge technologies actually contribute to the vigor that certain forms of folklore, including modern legends, enjoy today. While legends such as the mall kidnapping may be incorporated into television programs, films, and newspapers, the creation and maintenance of legends do not occur in a passive medium. A folk legend depends on an interactive mode of communicating that involves participants in a performance, in the give- and -take of face-to-face interaction.

As an active, vital form of traditional expressive behavior that is continually being created and re-created (folklore, if you will), modern legends have widespread appeal. For instance, the graphic violence of films such as the *Nightmare on Elm Street* or *Friday the Thirteenth* series is in sharp contrast to the horror that people can create in their imaginations as they listen to a tale unwind. Static images of the filmmaker cannot compare to the private hells that we can conjure in our minds as we connect the narrator's words to our particular fears and apprehensions, our own unique situations. The legend's narrator typically provides only the bare bones of a story, allowing the details to emerge both individually and communally as the audience engages in the legend process. The special appeal that modern legends have for young adults will be addressed shortly. Now, we need to take a step back and consider the realm of storytelling.

Myths, Folktales, and Legends
The inclination to tell stories may be a natural human impulse, for it is both universal and ancient. Every known human culture has a tradition of storytelling, and even the oldest preserved examples of writing include fabulous tales (which probably were circulating by word of mouth before they were written down). A reasonable guess is that storytelling and language developed at the same time. Of course, there are no historical records of our first storyteller's debut, but we can imagine how this performance might have unfolded.

Returning to camp from an unsuccessful hunting trip, Kent is startled by a woolly mammoth. With no time to think, Kent runs from the beast. He stumbles, but the accident is lucky because it allows Kent to avoid a hidden cliff. However, the enormous animal's momentum carries it to its death. Kent butchers the mammoth with newly flaked flints and carries the prime parts back to camp. There, he recounts his narrow escape in the language of his band, omitting some details and elaborating here and there. The accident becomes a deliberate act, a brave and clever trick to lure the creature over the cliff. Kent enjoys the reactions of his band as his tale unwinds. He glows with a new self-esteem.

While this scene is imaginary, the process of storytelling is still very much with us and has been well documented, researched, and interpreted. Like Kent's yarn, folk stories (or narratives) are a vehicle for communicating experience—experience understood in a broad sense, ranging from direct contact with the facts of life (hunting, danger, death) to encounters with the emotions, meanings, and mysteries of life (luck, self-esteem, and, again, death). Human cultures have invented many varieties of narratives to cover this broad spectrum of experience.

Myths, for example, explain the origins of the present-day world and are regarded by the community as both true and sacred. In myths, culture heroes and gods battle in an ancient universe as they create our world. The ancient Greeks had many stories about how Zeus, the father of heaven, reigned over his often disobedient family of Mount Olympus as he controlled events, both natural and supernatural. Modern American myths are more secular than religious, yet they still have their origins in the creation of a new world out of a wilderness. Pervasive themes in these newer myths take for granted America's manifest destiny, depicting an earthly paradise, a land of opportunity, a land of the free, and a home of the brave. George Washington, Ben Franklin, Davy Crockett, and Horatio Alger stand in place of Zeus, Apollo, Odysseus, and Theseus.

Folktales, on the other hand, are not taken literally (except perhaps by very young children). We leave reality behind us, suspend our disbelief, as we enter an unspecified never-never land. These folktales or *Märchen* (folklorists prefer the German term over the more popular but misleading *fairy tale*) are rigidly structured, single-stranded tales in which stock, well-known characters confront one another in tried-but-true settings. Weaker but fundamentally good characters eventually triumph over stronger but wicked foes, usually with the assistance of supernatural forces, and live happily ever after. "Cinderella" and "Jack in the Beanstalk" are two traditional folktales that have circulated orally and in print for many generations and, more recently, in film. Even modern mass-media stories such as the *Star Wars* trilogy draw heavily on the traditional plots, themes, formulas, and motifs of the older folktales.

A third major category of folk narrative is legend. The truth of events depicted in legends usually is open to question and debate. While the historical setting of a legend gives it an air of truth, its central incident occupies the shadowy region between the possible and the impossible. Loose and shifting in narrative form, legends revolve around a repeated idea or image that may be variously supernatural, miraculous, bizarre, eerie, horrible, disgusting, inexplicable, or embarrassing but is always memorable and worth repeating. Legend, unlike myth and folktale, is essentially a conversational form that, as Elliot Oring has written, "requires the audience to examine their world view, their sense of the normal, the boundaries of the natural, their conception of fate, destiny, and coincidence."

Long and complex stories such as the ancient myths and folktales are relatively unimportant in the oral literature of contemporary Americans. Current forms of spoken narrative are jokes, personal experience stories, and legends, especially the kind of legend termed *urban* or, more suitably, *modern.* Jan Brunvand, a leading scholar of these legends, defines them as "realistic stories concerning recent events (or alleged events) with an ironic or supernatural twist."

Modern Legends as Folklore

Many of these modern legends can be grouped according to their central themes. The child snatcher fits a wider theme of contemporary fearful figures, including the Hook, Fingernail Freddie, and the killer in the back seat. Another currently circulating group of stories (a *cycle*, in the folklorist's vocabulary) is based on the theme of contaminated food. Among young children, a certain brand of bubble gum is avoided because it is supposed to contain spider eggs. Older children and young adults may recall the rumor-turned-legend that a certain fast-food chain's hamburgers were actually wormburgers. Many of us probably are familiar with the batter-fried rat legend and the even older story of the mouse in the soda bottle.

Folklorists have several ways of studying these oral narratives. One basic approach is comparative: a story is compared with similar stories that have been passed on by word of mouth, have found their way into printed media such as newspapers or magazines, or have been included in short stories or novels. The purpose of comparative study is to learn something about the legend's past, how it is put together, and what it means. Comparing a collected text (that is, an oral story that has been written down word for word) to other similar texts also assists the folklorist in deciding whether the story is indeed a *folk* narrative. To make that decision, a folklorist asks the following questions:

Is the story *traditional?* Has it been circulating for some time? Does it have an identifiable history?

Is the story found in *variation?* Have different versions of the story been collected? (Different versions often are created through a process called localization, where various communities or groups of people change a story's details to suit their own circumstances.)

Has the story circulated primarily by means of *oral tradition,* that is, by word of mouth?

Is the story's author or originator *anonymous* or unknown? (One could say that, in a sense, such stories are community property in that they are continually being shaped and reshaped by the community as they spread from one person to the next.)

Answering yes to the questions above means that the story under consideration passes the test and can properly be called a folk narrative.

The mouse-in-the-soda-bottle story cycle demonstrates the characteristics of folk narrative just described. Certainly, the story has been circulating long enough to be considered traditional. A folklorist who investigated this tale found that as early as 1914, in Mississippi, a suit was brought against the Jackson Coca-Cola Bottling Company by a person claiming to have found a mouse drowned in his bottle of Coke. Since that time, at least 45 other court cases can be cited where mice were alleged to have been found in soft drink bottles, and, of course, a much larger number of localized, anonymous versions of the story has been collected from oral circulation.

In a more recent case (summer 1988), a Florida man claimed to have found a mouse in his beer can. After a necropsy was performed on the mouse, showing that the mouse had died *after* the beer was canned and that the rodent was likely shoved into the small opening, the man admitted he put the mouse in the can, hoping for a $35,000 settlement from the beer company. This particular example of the legend cycle demonstrates the circular nature of the relationship between legend and reality: art imitates life and life imitates art. This legend cycle also shows that there is no reason to assume that *all* modern legends are fictional. The relationship between legend and historical fact must be examined on a case-by-case basis.

Folk Motifs in New Settings

Even more comparisons can be made in the wider cycle of contamination legends. There is a strong narrative tradition whose central motif is the existence of alien creatures, especially snakes, inside a person's body. Folklorists have collected many tales about snakes being removed from people, and there is even an entire set of magical rites to cause snakes, lizards, or salamanders to form inside a person, as well as another set intended to get rid of them. A Hungarian *Märchen* (Aarne-Thompson no. 890A*) and a German ballad (Child no. 95, "Losgekaufte") tell the story of a young girl who has a snake in her bosom. In succession, each of her relatives refuses to help remove it. Finally, her lover finds the snake, which turns to gold.

The folk tradition of the bosom serpent also appears in both the literary and popular media. Nathaniel Hawthorne's short story entitled "Egotism; or the Bosom Serpent" centers around "a family peculiarity" passed along in the unfortunate Elliston lineage—the tendency to form snakes inside one's body. As we might expect of a Hawthorne tale, the actual existence of the snake is never confirmed, and the moral and symbolic aspects assume more importance than the story itself. Scholars have discovered that the bosom serpent motif circulated in newspapers as early as 1828, several years before the appearance of Hawthorne's story. To find recent use of this motif, one has to look no farther than the "chest buster" scene in the film *Aliens* or than the novel *The Doll Who Ate His Mother* by Robert Bloch (author of *Psycho*).

The more inclusive theme of alien creatures is widespread in folklore, literature, and mass media. The modern legend about baby alligators growing to monstrous size after being flushed into the sewer, for example, can be found in Thomas Pynchon's novel *V*, Harlan Ellison's short story "Croatoan" (in his collection *Strange Wine*), and the recent horror movie (released on video cassette) *Alligator*.

Modern Legends in Cultural Context

Legends also are studied in their cultural context, that is, the system of beliefs, attitudes, symbols, and conduct shared by a group of people. Assuming that a group's narratives reflect its way of life, the folklorist analyzes the narratives to determine which cultural elements are being brought to the fore in any particular legend or legend cycle. The content of legends changes over time and varies from culture to culture. While both colonial and modern legends, for example, often center around fear, the nature of the threat has changed over the years. Supernatural elements such as witches, vampires, vengeful spirits, and ghost ships inhabit earlier frightening legends. The fear in modern legends is generated by adversaries found in the rational world of everyday life: kidnappers, demented murderers, and impersonal institutions are today's enemies.

Contaminated food stories, for instance, point to feelings of powerlessness and mistrust on the part of the modern American consumer. Once in our history, we were close to all aspects of the food-producing process, from sowing and harvesting to preservation and preparation. Where family, neighbors, or at least acquaintances were involved in the process, we now rely on nameless and faceless workers. A by-product of automation and specialization is a sense that we have lost control over this basic element in our lives. To remain emotionally secure in our daily consumption of food—about whose actual history we are ignorant—requires no small measure of faith in anonymous strangers and institutions. Recurring tales of contaminated food—like repeated stories of calculating child snatchers or insane killers—reveal an underlying uneasiness about, and a sense of separation from, some of the basic institutions of our modern industrialized society. In our legends, as in our culture, fear of the unknown has shifted from supernatural sources to causes that, while explicable, remain beyond our control. As our legends continue to remind us, we are still helpless.

Modern Legends and Young Adults

Because American young adults occupy a never-never land between childhood and full-fledged adulthood, their needs and concerns and, thus, their folklore reflect such uncertainties. As their bodies and minds grow and change and they emerge from the protection afforded to children, young adults confront new feelings and begin to question the adult world they will soon be expected to join. Modern legends afford them an opportunity to deal with the hopes, fears, values, pitfalls, and inconsistencies of that world (which frequently they suppress) from the safe venue of words, often in ways that are socially and artistically satisfying. Modern legends simultaneously furnish vicarious experiences of the adult world and create a sense of solidarity among those who share similar concerns.

While the stories themselves may be entertaining, they can fulfill a variety of other functions; that is, they may have meaning at different levels. For example, modern legends warn of dangers found beyond the security of home (do not leave young children unattended in public places; look before you climb into your car or eat manufactured food), offer solutions to problems (perhaps it is best *not* to park in lovers' lane because the Hook and his ilk still roam there), or reinforce cultural rules (crime does not pay, as the would-be burglar in "The Choking Doberman" learned). Certainly not least, a legend-telling session, where knowledge is power and the ability to communicate is valued, provides a stage where performers have an opportunity to heighten their social status.

In the final analysis, perhaps modern legends are particularly appealing to young adults because the stories are part of their own folklore, that stable nucleus of legends, jokes, customs, gestures, speech, games, dances, and beliefs that is learned from other young adults rather than from adults or books. Adolescent folklore, like children's folklore, is tenacious, creative, strong, vital, and basically conservative (both structurally and morally). Although the dissemination of modern legends crosscuts generational lines, adolescents are especially fond of hearing and telling these stories. The legends that are in circulation at any time are those that young people have deemed sufficiently interesting, relevant, or gratifying to tell and tell again. Not only are the protagonists of many of these stories teenagers, the themes themselves are of central concern to young adults. Jan Harold Brunvand, for instance, has isolated the following themes in his books on urban legends: automobiles, teenage horrors, dreadful contaminations, purloined corpses and fear of the dead, dalliance, nudity and nightmares, sex and scandal, crime, and personalities.

Just as participating in the modern legend process can help young adults bridge the gap between childhood and adulthood, examining their own folklore (beginning with the familiar by looking at insider rather than outsider culture) can become a bridge to understanding what goes on in other cultural groups.

Further Reading

A recent excellent introductory discussion of folk narratives appears in Elliot Oring, *Folk Groups and Folklore Genres: An Introduction* (1986), Chapter 6: "Folk Narratives." Oring includes bibliographic notes and suggestions for further reading. The standard comparative references for folk narrative research are Antii Aarne, *The Types of the Folktale: A Classification and Bibliography* (2d rev. ed. 1964) and Stith Thompson, *Motif-Index of Folk-Literature*, 6 vols. (rev. ed. 1955).

For a readable discussion of American legends (with numerous examples and illustrations and a bibliography), see Richard M. Dorson, *America in Legend: Folklore from the Colonial Period to the Present* (1973). While Dorson's approach is historical, presenting legends in relation to broad themes of American history (e.g., "The Religious Impulse," "The Democratic Impulse"), the comparative and cultural contexts are clearly evident. The final chapter (focusing on "The Humane Impulse"), including sections on "Folklore of the Youth Culture," "Druglore," and "Draft Dodgers," is, of course, dated, but still illuminates the link between folklore and culture in the 1960s.

Jan Harold Brunvand is the reigning expert on modern legends (which he terms *urban legends*). His first book, *The Vanishing Hitchhiker: American Urban Legends and Their Meanings* (1981), is by far his best regarding analysis and interpretation of the legends. Included are a glossary of terms used in legend study, brief discussions of legends in their cultural context and of how to collect and study legends, and comprehensive notes on sources and references. *The Choking Doberman and Other "New" Urban Legends* (1984) is short on interpretation but includes a good bibliography. *The Mexican Pet: More "New" Urban Legends and Some Old Favorites* (1986) and *Curses! Broiled Again! The Hottest Urban Legends Going* (1989) are compilations of texts, many from popular or mass media sources, with minimal discussion. Two books by Alvin Schwartz, *Scary Stories to Tell in the Dark* (1981) and *More Scary Stories to Tell in the Dark* (1984), contain numerous modern legends and include annotations and a bibliography.

Stephen King's *Danse Macabre* (2d ed. 1981) provides a fascinating—if somewhat personal—view of horror and terror in a variety of fictional genres including short story, novel, radio, television, film, and, here and there, oral tradition. Although King concentrates on post-war examples, he does include some of the classics (notably, *Frankenstein, Dr. Jekyll and Mr. Hyde,* and *Dracula*). King's appendixes, listing a number of films and books, should be helpful in locating mass media treatments of legendary motifs.

A recent book by Harold Schechter, *The Bosom Serpent: Folklore and Popular Art* (1988), focuses on the use of folklore in popular art, including books, comics, tabloids, and films, tracing some folk motifs through the past two centuries.

Overall Theme to Be Explored

Michael Bell's essay considers the universal attraction that modern legends and contemporary folklore hold for all of us. It demonstrates that some motifs have reappeared time and time again, with only slight variations needed to make them current.

Storytelling is common to all cultures and eras. In this unit, we will look at the roles of horror and humor in the storytelling tradition. Why do people enjoy being scared? Why do monsters, ghosts, and vampires continue to enthrall us? We will also look at the black humor found in the joke cycles that appear almost immediately after every major catastrophe such as the *Challenger* tragedy, the Chernobyl disaster, and the Armenian earthquake. The unit also examines how scholars collect and test the validity of modern legends and relate new legends to the existing oral tradition, using the following humanities disciplines: literature; folklore; language and linguistics; history; and anthropology. You can approach these disciplines using the following questions:

What do these legends mean?

What do these legends tell us about our times? Ourselves? Do they sometimes express a feeling of alienation from society?

What need do legends satisfy in tellers and listeners?

Are these legends reflections of earlier themes in legends? Or do they represent specific characteristics unique to today's society?

How do they express present values, beliefs, and concerns?

Is the oral tradition less important now than it has been in the past?

What is the relationship between legend and historical fact?

Are folk legends sometimes reworked as literature?

What do these legends say about our culture? What cultural elements dominate in these tales?

How do myths, legends, and folktales differ from each other?

Do folk legends depict morality?

Why do some motifs (for example, food contamination) reappear throughout history?

How do scholars determine what is a true contemporary legend?

What is the universal appeal of the horror story? What need does it satisfy?

Do modern legends reflect society's hopes and anxieties?

What is the relationship between oral tradition and language?

How do topical jokes reflect our society's concerns?

Programs by Topic

The programs described on the following pages are arranged by topic: "What Is a Modern Legend?"; "Catastrophic Humor"; "Fear of the Supernatural"; "Collecting Modern Legends"; and "American Folklore." A specific format is suggested for each one, and some guidelines are included for structuring the discussion to ensure that the program has a humanities focus. The last sections of the unit provide suggestions for books, films, and videos that might be used in programming.

Any of these programs probably would be just one of a series, which could take a number of different forms. A broad series topic, for example, could be the "Nature of Narrative," exploring stories in many contexts historically, cross-culturally, and in terms of forms (from Greek myths to modern legends, from the "true" stories of historians and journalists to the "suspension of disbelief" necessary to both folktales and novels). A tighter focus might be "Narratives in the Modern World" and could include programs on contemporary forms of oral narrative, including modern legends, personal experience stories, and jokes.

As you can see, many program ideas can come from a single topic. Considering jokes, for instance, can lead to exploration of humor more generally: What is funny, and why? Again, such a topic can be seen in terms of different media (oral, written, film, etc.), different eras, and different cultures.

TOPIC: What Is a Modern Legend? I

Title: "Rumor Roulette: The Modern Legend Game."

Format: A game patterned after the TV game show "Wheel of Fortune."

Humanities Focus: This particular program introduces the modern legend as a genre of verbal folklore. It would be a good beginning program for a series. Attention is focused on important features of modern legends, including their content (the themes and motifs incorporated into them), their structure, their meanings, uses, and functions, and the criteria necessary for a legend to remain in oral tradition. Subsequent programs on modern legends might have participants collecting similar stories from their friends and then analyzing and annotating them or exploring the use of these themes and motifs in other narrative forms such as short stories, novels, and films.

Scholar's Questions and Comments: What is a legend? The scholar will give examples, elicit versions from the YAs, and abstract (through discussion) the characteristics of modern legends, including content, structure, and meaning.

Regarding the content of legends, the scholar will discuss their themes and motifs. Themes are the broad topics addressed in the legends; of course, these themes overlap and are found in various combinations. Motifs are the individual building blocks of stories (the characters, objects, and actions). Widespread themes include the following:

Contaminated food: spider egg bubble gum; pop rocks; wormburgers; Kentucky Fried Rat; mouse in Coke bottle; Mickey Moust LSD.

Fearful figures: Mall kidnapper; the Hook; Fingernail Freddie; killer in the back seat; alligators in the sewer; hairy-armed hitchhiker; the licked hand.

Crime: choking doberman; severed fingers.

Aliens in the body (medical horrors): bosom serpent; spider eggs in sore; spider in the hairdo; poison dress.

Unfortunate pets: poodle in the microwave (cf., baby roast); dead cat in bag; Mexican pet; dog in the Chinese restaurant.

Famous people: Michael Jackson's phone number; death of Little Mikey; Cabbage Patch Doll tragedy; Reggie Jackson in the elevator; vanishing hitchhiker (as Jesus, etc); Elvis is alive.

How are legends put together (i.e., what is their structure)? Although modern legends are loosely structured, they usually contain various combinations of the following elements:

Announcement: This indicates that some sort of narrative is to follow. The announcement often provides the setting, time, place, and characters involved. Examples: "I just heard the weirdest thing." "Have you heard about what happened . . . ?" "There was an article in the newspaper about. . . ." "This is a true story. A woman went shopping at the mall. . . ."

Verification/affirmation of truth: Often there is a statement that lends credence to or supports the truth of what is to follow (or, sometimes, what has just been related). Sources for verification include friends and relatives, newspapers, and television.

Conflict and resolution: Typically, a person is confronted with a situation that is dangerous, distasteful, or embarrassing. In short, an anxiety-producing situation exists. The resolution is, at best, usually a return to equilibrium (by riddance of the problem); sometimes, the resolution leaves the protagonist in a worse situation.

Statement of meaning (moral): There may be a moral tag near or at the end of the story, a summary of the meaning from the narrator's point of view: Crime doesn't pay; you never know what's in the food you eat; there are lots of crazy people out there; cleanliness is next to Godliness; some people are really stupid; you have to keep your eye on your kids; we're powerless in the modern world; don't judge a book by its cover. Where the announcement alerts listeners that they are about to hear a story (separating what is to follow from ordinary conversation), the moral tag closes the narrative.

Meanings, uses, and functions of legends: Why do people circulate these stories? What are some of the cultural functions of legends (such as entertainment, education, validation of certain standards, relief of tension or fear).

The Game

1. Divide the participants into several groups.
2. Each group spins the wheel three times to determine:
   a. Announcement
   b. Verification statement
   c. Theme
3. Compose a modern legend based on the traditional pattern discussed (this is called communal creation).
4. One member of each group (the designated storyteller) tells the legend.
5. A panel of YAs discusses the Process of Oral Tradition, and decides which newly composed legends shall live on in oral tradition. The panel will use the following criteria for making judgments: Is the story memorable and worth repeating (the textual criterion)? Does the story have a potential use, function, or meaning (the contextual criterion)? Does the story lend itself to a convincing, aesthetically pleasing performance (the aesthetic criterion)?
6. A follow-up activity might be to have the YAs circulate the legends that pass the test outlined in 5, above. They should tell one other YA and one adult and see how long the legend takes to return to them.

TOPIC: What Is a Modern Legend? II

The food contamination motif will be used to illustrate a type of legend that keeps appearing in updated versions.

Program Title: "Don't Eat That."

Format: Skit/lecture. YAs will act out past and current food fears (for example, Wormburgers).

Humanities Focus: The skits will be placed in a historical context, and the basis for these stories will be explored in relation to contemporary values and concerns.

Scholar's Questions and Comments: The scholar will comment on why some folk motifs have continued appeal and discuss how these motifs are adapted to each era. The scholar could also discuss the loss of control over a basic element of life—food. Questions should include: What fears are expressed by these stories? What is the cause of these fears? How has the motif changed to accommodate contemporary mores and beliefs? What has caused us to lose trust in the quality of various types of foods? Where does this distrust come from? What is the underlying cause for it?

YA Involvement: As part of this program, YAs would be asked to share examples of food taboos that are currently circulating. They might also ask their parents for versions of these types of stories and legends in their day. YAs will act out food legends in skits.

Topic: Folk Humor

Joke cycles will be considered part of oral tradition.

Program Title: Use the punch line of a current joke.

Format: Lecture/discussion.

Humanities Focus: A scholar in folklore will explain how these types of jokes evolve and how they spread so rapidly. The scholar will lead the audience in discussing why we seem to need this type of humor.

Scholar's Questions and Comments: Why do we laugh at disasters? Are these types of jokes traditional? What types of incidents create these jokes? What is the historical significance of joke cycles? How have these jokes changed over time? What do they really mean?

YA Involvement: The scholar will ask YAs to share recent jokes they have heard about catastrophes and disasters.

Topic: Fear of the Supernatural I

Program Title: "Fearsome Fiends."

Format: Program series with several components: reading and discussion; a film series of modern monsters; an exhibit of horror posters from movies; and a costume pageant of frightening creatures.

Humanities Focus: The scholar will explore with audiences the tradition of horror found in folklore and literature as demonstrated through the various program formats. The need for fictional horror in our lives will be discussed.

> Scholar's Questions and Comments: What role have monsters played in history? In literature?
> Have our fears of the supernatural changed? Or do they remain basically the same?
> Why do we enjoy being frightened?
> What do costumes and masks symbolize?
> Does the creation of an image of our fears (for example, a were-wolf) help us cope with these fears?

YA Involvement: YAs could take part in the pageant and help prepare the costumes.

Promotion: Hold the last program on Halloween.

Books and Films: Frankenstein; Dracula; Dr. Jekyll and Mr. Hyde; The Fly (both film versions); *Godzilla; Painted Door.*

TOPIC: Fear of the Supernatural II

Program Title: "See Ya Later, Alligator—Reptilian Creatures in Legends."

Format: Reading and discussion program of the reptile legend in literature.

Humanities Focus: The scholar will comment on this phenomenon in literature and in current legends and lead a discussion on the meaning of this concept.

Scholar's Questions and Comments: What do legends of this type represent? Are they based on some kind of universal fear? If so, of what? Are they based on actual events? How is the reptile motif used in literature? Have you heard any versions of this legend?

Books: Thomas Pynchon, *V;* Harlan Ellison, *Strange Wine;* J. D. Salinger, *Catcher in the Rye;* Nathaniel Hawthorne, *Egotism;* or *The Bosom Serpent.*

TOPIC: Fear of the Supernatural III

Program Title: "Who's Going to Get You?"

Format: Lecture and discussion with a panel of YAs as reactors.

Humanities Focus: The scholar will demonstrate how recurring characters (the vanishing hitchhiker, the Hook, etc.) give people a chance to experience emotions and fears in a safe setting. The persistence of these legends and their variations will be discussed.

Scholar's Questions and Comments: How do these legendary figures relate to the real threats in modern society? Do imaginary figures of horror provide us with a safeguard? If so, what is it? How are masks in primitive cultures similar to these legendary figures? Why do the same characters turn up again and again?

Note: A variation on this theme might be "Places to Dread," which would identify certain sites that are traditionally considered dangerous (haunted houses, morgues, etc.). The scholar would discuss what, if any, causes might form the historical basis for this fear.

TOPIC: Collecting Modern Legends

Title: "When Is a Story a Modern Legend?"

Format: A panel of scholars will lead a discussion of modern legends based on historical roots. Scholars will comment on their methods of investigating their subject matter. This would be followed by a discussion with the audience on current variations of legends.

Humanities Focus: The purposes of the workshop will be to demonstrate how the scholars collect and validate legends and to introduce YAs to the scholars' working methods.

Scholar's Questions and Comments: YAs will share and swap popular modern legends. They could also be asked to elicit versions of these legends from older generations. The scholar's questions will cover the following:

Truth or fiction? Are modern legends literal accounts of actual events? Could such strange events have taken place in so many localities and happened to so many different people? Do the structure and content (i.e., motifs) of these stories point toward truth or fiction?

Why are these stories told? Stories may not be factual but still contain truths (one begins to sense those "larger questions" looming). Do the stories reflect current concerns? What concerns are evident?

Searching humanities collections for other stories. What kinds of stories have been passed down over the generations? What are the differences among legends, myths, folktales, and fairy tales, or Märchen? If these urban legends are indeed legends, how do they differ from other sorts of legends? Are there legends that are specific to a community? Do they center on certain places? Characters? Do they explain the origins of names of local places? Do families have stories concerning an cestors? Looking at folk narratives from a larger perspective, are there changes in the content of legends over time? Do the changes correlate to larger cultural and social changes? Are stories that have been collected in other parts of the world (such as Africa or Europe) substantially different from American versions? Why or why not?

YA Involvement: The YAs should bring in current versions of jokes or motif stories.

TOPIC: American Folklore

Program Title: "The Truth behind the Legend."

Format: Series of programs based on *America in Legend* by Richard M. Dorson. Storytellers will tell or sing the legends. Then scholars and folklorists will discuss the relationship of these legends to American history.

Humanities Focus: The scholar will consider Dorson's premise that American folklore follows history by growing out of the major philosophies of each era (religious, democratic, economic, etc.).

Scholar's Questions and Comments: Are folk legends a popular form of history? How do they express the issues and concerns of society? What role do they play in interpreting history to the general public?

Book: Richard M. Dorson, *America in Legend.*

A Sample Bibliography

The following bibliography suggests popular reading for young adults on the subjects of modern legends, myths, and folklore.

Abels, Harriette. *The Loch Ness Monster.* Crestwood House, 1987.

Possible sightings of the monster, accompanied by black-and-white photographs, are described, and theories concerning its existence are explored.

Addams, Charles. *Creature Comforts.* Simon & Schuster, 1981.

From a window washer perched in King Kong's hairy palm to a witch piloting a flying candy cottage, Addams' cartoon roundup is a gleeful melange of silliness and the macabre.

Aldiss, Brian W. *Frankenstein Unbound.* Random, 1974.

Former presidential adviser Joe Bodenland is thrust from 2020 America to 1816 Switzerland where the Shelleys and Lord Byron share equal reality with Mary Shelley's fictional Victor Frankenstein and his mother.

Bradbury, Ray. *Something Wicked This Way Comes*. Simon & Schuster; Bantam, 1962.

Two curious boys in a small midwestern town become the quarry of the sinister Mr. Dark when they visit the Cooger & Dark Pandemonium Shadow Show.

Card, Orson Scott. *The Seventh Son*. Tor, 1987.

In an alternate early nineteenth-century America where folk magic works, Alvin Miller is born, the seventh son of a seventh son, capable of powerful magic—and somebody or something does not want him to grow up. *Red Prophet* is the sequel.

Estey, Dale. *A Lost Tale*. St. Martin's; Berkley, 1980.

Druids and a unicorn on the Isle of Man help Brigid protect the wounded German soldier she loves.

Gardner, John. *Grendel*. Knopf; Ballantine, 1971.

Heroic Beowulf becomes the villain in this retelling of the Beowulf legend.

Garner, Alan. *The Owl Service*. Walck; Ballantine, 1968.

Two teenage boys in a Welsh valley love the same girl, and as their intense feelings mount, they find themselves acting out an age-old legend of love and revenge.

Gunning, Thomas G. *Strange Mysteries*. Dodd, 1987.

Among these ten true tales of strange and puzzling happenings are those of a dolphin that guides ships through perilous waters, a pigeon that carries secret coded messages, lighthouse keepers who disappear, and buried treasure that is never recovered.

Hamilton, Virginia. *Sweet Whispers, Brother Rush*. Putnam; Avon, 1982.

Tree sees her uncle's ghost, who takes her to the past, where she discovers harsh secrets about her mother.

Hoover, H. M. *The Dawn Palace*. Dutton, 1988.

Hoover retells the Medea story from a feminist perspective, making Jason the monster.

Irving, Washington. *The Legend of Sleepy Hollow*. 1818–1820. Various editions.

Superstitious school teacher Ichabod Crane rides home after hearing ghost stories and is certain he meets the Headless Horseman.

Jackson, Shirley. *We Have Always Lived in the Castle*. Viking, 1962.

Constance Blackwood is acquitted by the jury for poisoning her family but six years later is still judged guilty by her neighbors and thus is trapped in her home.

James, Henry. *Turn of the Screw*. 1891.

A governess tries to break the spell she believes evil spirits have cast over the two innocent children in her care.

King, Stephen. *Pet Sematary*. Doubleday; NAL, 1983.

Chicagoan Louis Creed and his family move to a new house only to discover that it backs up on a local graveyard for pets—which backs up on a second graveyard from which dead people return.

King, Stephen. *Salem's Lot*. Doubleday; NAL, 1975.

The streets of Jerusalem's Lot, Maine, are deserted in the daytime, but they come alive at night when the villagers turn into vampires.

Larson, Gary. *The Far Side Gallery 2*. Andrews, McMeel & Parker, 1986.

"Polly wanna finger?" asks the portly matron as she plunges a digit into the parrot's cage. This is a taste of the talents of the newest king of macabre cartooning.

Lawrence, Louise. *The Earth Witch*. Harper; Ace, 1981.

Trying to help a bitter, middle-aged recluse, Welsh teenager Owen becomes her lover when she grows younger and more beautiful in the spring; by winter's eve, she is a hideous old hag demanding his life in sacrifice for her bounty.

Lillington, Kenneth. *The Selkie*. Harper, 1985.

Convinced that Fiona is really a selkie (a legendary seal-woman), Cathy Gascoyne teams up with a young handyman to find the selkie's missing magical skin.

Llewelyn, Morgan. *The Horse Goddess*. Houghton, 1982.

When the daughter of a Celtic chief flees the priesthood by running away with a band of Asia Minor horsemen, she is stalked by her tribe's chief priest, who appears in the form of a giant ghost wolf.

Lovecraft, H. P. *Bloodcurdling Tales of Horror and the Macabre: The Best of H. P. Lovecraft*. Ballantine, 1982.

A collection of some of Lovecraft's best-known tales introduces the horrific monsters that populate the author's mystical Cthulku Mythos.

McIntyre, Vonda N. *The Bride*. Dell, 1985.

McIntyre's sympathetic portrayal of Dr. Frankenstein's monster, Victor, and Eva, the beautiful bride brought to life and coveted by the manic Frankenstein, becomes a tender love story with a bittersweet ending.

McKinley, Robin. *Beauty: A Retelling of the Story of Beauty and the Beast*. Harper; Pocket, 1978.

This elegantly styled romance extends the fairy tale characters into a fully imagined world.

Mansfield, Sue and Mary Bowen Hall. *Some Reasons for War*. Harper, 1988.

From Alexander the Great to Rambo, the authors examine myths that glorify war and good guy/bad guy stereotypes that fuel aggression.

Myers, Walter Dean. *The Legend of Tarik*. Viking; Scholastic, 1981.

In a legendary medieval story set in North Africa, a black knight frees oppressed people from an evil tyrant.

Peck, Richard. *The Ghost Belonged to Me*. Viking; Dell, 1975.

Thirteen-year-old Alexander teams up with his great-uncle and a spidery-legged girl named Blossom to put to rest the soggy remains of a drowned girl who haunts Alexander. Follow-up adventures include *The Dreadful Future of Blossom Culp*.

Pierce, Meredith Ann. *The Darkangel*. Atlantic Monthly Press; Tor, 1982.

This and its sequel, *A Gathering of Gargoyles*, spin an eerie fantasy about Aeriel, who falls in love with a vampire who steals the souls of his many brides.

Pizer, Vernon. *Eat the Grapes Downward*. Dodd, 1983.

This is an entertaining assortment of beliefs, myths, legends, and anecdotes about humankind's gustatory pursuits and vagaries.

Poe, Edgar Allen. *Tales and Poems of Edgar Allan Poe*. Macmillan, 1963.

The outstanding tales of mystery and suspense from the pen of one of the great mystery writers of all time.

Pynchon, Thomas. *V.* Lippincott, 1963.

In this zany picture of life, Benny Profane (part of a crew patroling for alligators in the sewers of New York City) and his pals (the Whole Sick Crew) deliver a melancholy comment on the way things are now (not that they were *ever* any better).

Roueche, Berton. *Feral*. Harper; Avon, 1974.

A young couple seeking peace from city life set up housekeeping in a small town only to be terrorized by hostile, night-prowling bands of abandoned, starving cats.

Saberhage, Fred. *The Frankenstein Papers*. Baen; Simon & Schuster, 1986.

In a revisionist treatment of the Frankenstein story, the monster is a sensitive outsider in search of identity.

Shelley, Mary. *Frankenstein*. Illus. by Barry Moser. Univ. of California/ Penny Royal Press, 1984. (Many other editions available).

In this modern large-size edition, Moser's haunting woodcuts express the horror of the monster, as well as the suffering of the outsider driven away by those he would love.

Stoker, Bram. *Dracula*. 1898.

This classic vampire tale has spawned numerous short stories, novels, and movies.

Vampires: Two Centuries of Great Vampire Stories. Ed. by Alan Ryan. Doubleday, 1987.

Including the funny, the murky, and the downright horrific, this literate sampling crisscrosses 150 years of vampire lore.

Wakefield, Pat A. *A Moose for Jessica*. Dutton, 1987.

Marvelous photographs chronicle what happens when a bull moose wanders out of the woods during mating season and takes up with a Hereford cow named Jessica.

Wells, H. G. *Island of Dr. Moreau*. 1896.

Rescued from a shipwreck by a mysterious man, Edward Prendick is forced ashore, where he discovers that terrible experiments are being conducted by mad Dr. Moreau.

Werewolves: A Collection of Original Stories. Ed. by Jane Volen and Martin H. Greenberg. Harper, 1988.

Fifteen original stories capture the legendary beast in a host of strange and effective guises.

Wescott, Earle. *Winter Wolves*. Yankee Publishing, 1988.

In one of the coldest Maine winters ever, long-dead wolves threaten the residents of Steel Harbor.

Wilhelm, Kate. *Oh, Susannah!* Houghton; Berkley, 1982.

While he is falling in love with Susannah, a young woman stricken with an involuntary tall-tale-telling syndrome, graduate student Brad joins her in the hot pursuit of a self-propelled, roaming blue suitcase.

Wilson, F. Paul. *The Keep*. Morrow; Berkley, 1981.

Sent to garrison in an ancient castle in the Transylvania Mountains, a group of German soldiers discovers it shares the premises with a gruesome cadre of walking dead.

Wilson, F. Paul. *The Tomb*. Whispers; Jove, 1984.

An investigator uncovers a complicated scheme perpetrated by an Indian diplomat seeking revenge and hoping to appease his legendary goddess of destruction.

Appendix 1

Glossary of Frequently Used Terms

ACTIVITIES: The specific events that will be used to present a series of humanities programs. These might include lectures, discussions, special events, displays, and publications that would compose aspects of the total project.

FORMAT: A method or medium of program presentation (e.g., lecture, film, book discussion, walking tour, etc.). A list of possible program formats is included earlier in this book.

GOAL: The overall purpose of a project. Goals are not reachable, achievable, or measurable. (*See* OBJECTIVES)

HUMANIST/SCHOLAR: An individual professionally trained and involved in teaching, writing about, or researching one of the humanities disciplines, usually in an academic setting. For the purposes of NEH, scholars are required to have a terminal degree (Ph.D. or master's) in a discipline of the humanities. Scholars in the humanities will be involved in planning and implementing young adult programs.

HUMANITIES: Congress provides this definition: "The term humanities includes but is not limited to the study of: language, both modern and classical; linguistics, literature; history; jurisprudence; philosophy; archaeology; comparative religion, ethics; the history, criticism, theory and practice (not performance) of the arts; and those aspects of the social sciences which have humanistic content and employ humanistic method."

HUMANITIES PROGRAM: Program designed to increase public understanding of the humanities through (1) the discovery, the interpretation, and greater appreciation of the humanities disciplines and (2) the interaction of scholars and the general public, including young adults.

LIBRARY RESOURCE: Any resource owned by or available to the library that can be used to develop, present, or enhance humanities programs. This may include staff, special collections, media, space (meeting rooms), art works, special funds, and Friends and volunteer groups.

OBJECTIVES: The specific, planned outcomes of a project. Objectives form the framework for a project. They describe what it is hoped will be achieved by sponsoring the humanities program. Objectives are reachable, measurable, and achievable. (*See* GOAL)

PROGRAM: One or more events presented to the public, using a variety of formats that encourage discussion based on the humanities. A scholar should take part in some aspect of every program, either directly or through the planning process.

PROJECT: A series of planned activities designed by library staff and contributing scholars. The written description of the project plan becomes the proposal to request funds from NEH or the state humanities council.

TARGET AUDIENCE: The specific group that a library designs its program to reach. A target audience may be all young adults or a specific segment of young adults (e.g., twelve- to fourteen-year-olds, boys, ethnic minorities, etc.).

THEME: The overall idea or concept around which a program series is planned. For example, in the sample program "Courtly Love in the Shopping Mall," the theme is teenage courtship and love.

TOPIC: The focus around which a program is designed. A topic is more specific than a theme. For example, a program based on the "courtly love" theme may have as one of its topics fashion and courtship through the centuries.

YOUNG ADULT: In most libraries, defined as a person in junior or senior high school, roughly between twelve and eighteen years old.

Appendix 2

Goals and Objectives

Every decision is based on a set of underlying goals and objectives, whether they are verbalized or not. At their most effective, a project's goals and objectives can:

Clarify thinking
Communicate intent
Provide a foundation for later decision making
Facilitate evaluation of the project

As you develop goals and objectives, ask yourself these questions:

What are my reasons for having young adult humanities programs in the library?
How will these programs benefit my library?
How do these programs meet or conflict with the overall goals and objectives of the library?
How will these programs benefit the scholars and young adults who participate?
What future activities might these programs foster?

Remember that goals are long range and broad in scope, while objectives are short term and measurable. For example, you might see a goal for your programs as being: "To broaden the audience that the library serves." This broad goal can be divided into concrete, measurable objectives that are written in specific terms so that a criterion of success easily can be applied. Thus, one objective based on this goal might be: "Ten young adults who have not been library users will participate in this series of programs." And a second objective might be: "The planning committee will include representatives from diverse sections of the community, including young adults."

There are many other goals you could formulate for programs such as this. Another example: "To introduce young adults to the joy and excitement of the humanities." A goal for young adult participants could be: "To learn more about the relationship of the humanities to everyday life." Based on that goal, one objective might be: "At the end of these programs, the participant will be able to recognize and express the relevance of one or more of the humanities disciplines to his or her life." (You might even want to ask the participants to do this in your program evaluation.)

Appendix 3

Steps in Programming—An Outline

I. Background
  A. Information about your community
    1. Population, demographics (especially relating to youth)
    2. Historical and cultural climate
    3. Educational institutions
    4. Youth agencies
    5. Cultural agencies
    6. Political structure
    7. Organizations (civic, religious, social)
    8. Media
    9. Current events and topical interests
  B. Possible program topics
    1. Local interests
    2. Young adult interests (e.g., dating, rock music)
    3. ALA/YASD themes (e.g., love, heroes, legends)
    4. General trends or interests (e.g., AIDS, presidential elections, drug abuse, jobs)
  C. Resources available to develop it fully
    1. Library (e.g., books, tapes, films, art works, special collections, staff members)
    2. Community (e.g., museums, historical societies, theater groups, local resource people)
  D. If seeking NEH funds, describe how the humanities will be incorporated
  E. People who will help develop the theme
    1. Staff
    2. Planners (scholars and community members, including young adult representatives)
II. Planning the project
  A. Planning committee appointed
  B. Planning meetings (areas to be covered)
    1. Preliminary data gathered
    2. Audience to be reached
    3. Program objectives
    4. Selected topics for program
    5. Formats, presenters, additional scholars
    6. Future responsibilities of each committee member
    7. Scheduling of meetings and planning deadlines
    8. Series evaluation
    9. Budget

III. Describing the Program Series
  A. Title
  B. Theme/concept
  C. Program topics
  D. Audience
  E. Program formats
    1. Speakers
    2. Media
    3. Special events
    4. Exhibits and displays
    5. Schedule (dates and times)
  F. Evaluation/follow-up

Appendix 4

Project Personnel

It is important to have a clear understanding of what various members of the project staff do. It is especially necessary to provide job descriptions or lists of qualifications for the job of project director, contributing scholar, and any other staff you may hire as part of the project. If you are project director, you have the overall job of managing the project from start to finish, top to bottom; however, the responsibility is quite manageable, especially if you are able to delegate certain tasks to capable people, including planning committee members, scholars, and discussion leaders. It will help you, though, to know what to expect and what is expected of you. Even if you choose to hire (and supervise) the project director, the following short job description should be of assistance.

Job Description—Project Director
    Responsibilities:
    Selecting planning or advisory committee members
    Coordinating the development of the project and selecting related
        materials
    Selecting and coordinating scholars
    Selecting and coordinating others involved in the project
    Coordinating library staff and volunteers as related to the project
    Delegating responsibilities to committee members
    Distributing materials
    Developing a public relations campaign
    Preparing and managing the budget
    Managing each specific aspect of the project, including:
        Selecting and preparing site
        Introducing program, speakers, and others involved
        Wrap-up
        Paying honoraria and other bills
        Project evaluation
        Reporting to funding source and library governing authority
        Supervising project staff

Selecting Scholars

A major responsibility of the project director is selecting the scholars who will take part in a program. The following guidelines will help you select the right scholars for your project.

    Scholars may be, in a sense, the guest stars of each program. This includes all the benefits and problems star billing can cause. By selecting the right scholar, you have an invaluable resource who can offer insights into the material and deepen the humanities experience for the participants. And yet, you must choose a scholar not only for his critical ability, but also for his ability to understand his role in your program—that of equal partner with the project director and the participants. The scholar must be open to the unique concerns of the audience and be congenial and tactful in expressing his opinions, yet all the while he must serve the important responsibility of instruction.

Selecting the right scholars will be one of the most critical issues you will face during planning. Keeping in mind the responsibilities of and necessary qualifications for potential scholars, you can contact several sources to identify scholars. These include state humanities councils, colleges, universities, community colleges, museums, historical societies, and other librarians who have used scholars in library humanities projects.

After you have been given referrals, you might ask other people who have heard these scholars speak to give you an evaluation of the scholars' work and style. Department chairpersons might be a good source of information. You might even sit in on a lecture or class to get a feel for a scholar's style. Remember, you are asking the scholar to deal with a *nonacademic audience of young adults,* so the scholar's style while conducting a formal university class may be misleading.

Just as there are informal networks for other professions—publishing, medicine, law, librarianship—there are informal networks of humanities scholars. Once you tap into the scholar network, you are likely to find an abundance of good candidates. First, go to a source—another librarian with experience in humanities programming, for example, and discuss these scholars. After compiling a list of likely scholars, *talk* to them. Explain your project ideas. Ask for their help and *listen* to what they say. Are they really interested, and do they understand what you hope to accomplish with your programs?

Regardless of whom you choose as scholars, their success will depend, in great part, on how well you prepare them for their roles in your project. Try to provide each scholar with a profile of the intended young adult audience she will be working with—age and education levels, sex, social and economic backgrounds, and anticipated attendance figures. You should be able to provide this information as a result of all the planning you have done for your project.

Finally, be sure to make clear to the scholars exactly what you expect of them in terms of the services they are to perform (lecture, written reading guide, discussion leader, etc.). Put it all in writing, along with the details of honoraria, travel reimbursement, and program date, place, and time. The proceeding job description for a project humanities scholar will aid you in your scholar selection process.

Job Description—Scholar

Minimum qualifications:

Advanced degree in the humanities (a doctorate or sometimes a master's). Much depends on the topic, the other qualifications of the scholar, and the requirements of your funding agency. Professionally engaged in or retired from teaching, writing, research, or study in the humanities

Background appropriate to the specific programs being presented

Enthusiasm about public humanities programming

Time to fulfill the demands of the program

Preferred qualifications:

Experience in public programming in the humanities, especially in libraries

Understanding of young adults and enthusiasm about working with them in an out-of-school setting

Appendix 5

Putting Together the Budget

Budgeting for a project or series of programs is not an especially arduous or complex task. However, you will need to keep certain expenses in mind. To assist you in this, sample budget worksheets listing possible expense categories for a project follow. You will have to cost them out, using your own experience and local costs as a guide. Some of the items will not apply to your program, and you may have to add others.

As you begin your budget, keep these three things in mind.

1. It is wiser to overestimate than to underestimate costs.
2. Costs can change quickly; a budget must be kept current.
3. Donated services, facilities, equipment, or materials are as important as cash contributions. To see how in-kind contributions can be itemized in your budget, look at the in-kind contribution column on the worksheets and the sample in-kind contributions time log.

Sample Budget Worksheet

	Direct	In-Kind Contribution	Not Applicable

Staff and Volunteer Time
    Project director
    Planning committee members
    Library staff			

Honoraria
    Scholars
    Outside evaluator
    Graphic artist designing
        publicity			

Travel Expenses
    Scholar
    Other program presenters
    Evaluator			

Materials
    Distribution to all participants
    Complimentary copies
    Support materials for
        library collection
    Audiovisual materials			

(Continued)

	Direct	In-Kind Contribution	Not Applicable

Publicity
  Newspapers
  Radio
  Television			

Printing and Duplicating
  Duplication of materials
    for planning committee
  Duplication of materials
    for scholars and
    participants
  Printing of brochures,
    posters, fliers, fact
    sheets, news releases,
    and other promotional
    materials			

Postage
  Publicity materials
  Letters and materials to
    scholars and other program
    presenters
  Mailings to participants			

Meeting-room Facilities
Equipment Rental
  Audiovisual use
  Scholar use			

Refreshments
  For scholars and others
    before program
  For participants during
    program			

Contingencies
  Lodging in case of
    inclement weather
  Other			

In-Kind Contributions: Sample Time Log

Name: John Smith

Position: Planning Committee Member

Program: Courtly Love in the Shopping Mall

Dates Covered: 10/91 to 1/92

Date	Activity	Hours	Dollar Value (At $10/hour)
10/3/91	Planning committee meeting	3½	$35
10/12/91	Contacted possible funding sources	4	$40
10/17/91	Planning committee meeting	3½	$35
10/20–10/21/91	Reviewed theme and materials to be used in programs	9	$90
10/30/91	Planning committee meeting	3½	$35
12/31/91	Contacted community leaders to secure their support for and participation in programs	4	$40
1/16/92	Attended opening session as planning committee member and as participant	2½	$25
Total		30	$300

Index

Compiled by Kathleen J. Patterson

Evelyn Shaevel was executive director of ALA's Young Adult Services Division from 1975–1989. From 1985–1991 she developed and directed the YASD/NEH project and, along with Peggy O'Donnell, created the training materials which evolved into *Courtly Love in the Shopping Mall*. Shaevel has been director of Marketing for ALA Publishing since 1989. Previously she was a branch manager and assistant coordinator, Adult/Young Adult Services for the Lake County Public Library System in Indiana and a school librarian in Gary.

Peggy O'Donnell is a library consultant who served as principal project consultant for the YASD/NEH project, "Library Programming in the Humanities for Young Adults." Her varied experience includes serving as director of the ALA/NEH "Courses by Newspaper" project, as consultant on training for the ALA/NEH "Let's Talk about It" project, and as coordinator of continuing education at the Southwestern Library Association.

Susan Soloman Goldberg is director of the Minneapolis Public Library and Information Center. Before 1990, she served as Deputy Director and Coordinator of Adult and Young Adult Services at the Tucson Public Library. While there she developed or directed seven NEH-funded grant projects, including several for young people. From 1987–1989 Goldberg was managing director of the Arizona Theatre Company and toured the country as a member of the YASD/NEH Project Advisory Committee. She served as president of the Public Library Association in 1987–1988.

Rolly Kent's background ranges from teaching at the elementary, secondary and university levels to acting as director of the Tucson Writers' Project and the Tucson Writers' Conference. He has been involved in several NEH grant projects including "America: A Reading," "Voices and Visions," and "Behind the Scenes: Theatre and Tradition." Kent is a writer and poet. His published works include *Spirit, Hurry* (Confluence Press), *Queen of Dreams* (Simon & Schuster) and poetry published in many magazines including *Atlantic*, *Nation* and *Poetry* magazines.

OURTLY LOVE IN THE SHOPPING MALL ▪

Programming for Young Adults with a Humanities Focus

American Library Association • Young Adult Services Division • Funding Provided By A Grant From The National Endowment For The Humanities

Logo designed for the YASD/NEH project by Natalie Wargin